Sample Business Plans
Premier FastTrac

first edition

Courtney Price
R. Mack Davis
Richard H. Buskirk

Premier
Entrepreneur
Programs Inc
Denver, CO 80201

Also by Courtney Price, R. Mack Davis and Richard H. Buskirk

- The Entrepreneur's Handbook
- Program for Writing Winning Business Plans
- The Entrepreneur's Resource Handbook
- The Corporate Venturing Planning Handbook
- The Entrepreneur's FastTrac I Handbook
- The Entrepreneur's FastTrac II Handbook

First Edition

Copyright 1994 by Courtney Price, R. Mack Davis and Richard H. Buskirk

All Rights Reserved

Printed in the United States of America

ISBN 0-944303-15-3

Edited by Alys Novak

Interior Design by Creative Light

Table of Contents

I.   **INTRODUCTION** iv

CHAPTER 1

SWEET ALTERNATIVES

    Overview 1-1

    Critique 1-3

    Business Plan 1-7

CHAPTER 2

WILL BULLAS INCORPORATED

    Overview 2-1

    Critique 2-2

    Business Plan 2-5

CHAPTER 3

SIEMPRE ENVISIONS

    Overview 3-1

    Critique 3-3

    Business Plan 3-7

CHAPTER 4

EAST SIDE PLATING CO.

    Overview 4-1

    Critique 4-3

    Business Plan 4-8

SAMPLE BUSINESS PLANS

Introduction

Every business should be operated from a well-written and complete business plan. That is one of the key reasons all FastTrac II participants are required to write a business plan to graduate from the program. However, the process of writing a business plan is time consuming, frustrating, and ominous. It involves technical texts, explanations, descriptions, and financial statements. It's tough to start the process of writing your plan.

You will struggle over hundreds of questions such as:
> What type of information should I put into my plan?
> How much detail should I include?
> How should I document industry statistics?
> What format should I use to identify my major competitors?
> What type of information should be in chart or graph form?
> How do I explain the projections in my financial statements?
> How long should my plan be?

Premier FastTrac research has demonstrated that entrepreneurs learn quicker by interacting with each other, which is the reason for the networking sessions in every Premier FastTrac training program. They also learn faster how to write and design a business plan by having examples of well-constructed business plans to use as guides while preparing their plans.

Therefore, Premier FastTrac Sample Business Plans provides selected business plans for all FastTrac participants to use as models while preparing their business plan. Reviewing this book will save you countless hours and lots of frustration. It will show you how other FastTracers and students using The Entrepreneur's Planning Handbook, by Premier Entrepreneur Programs (PEP), have applied different techniques to make their plans easier to read and write. It will illustrate how various types of information can be attractively displayed to encourage the reader to continue reading the plan.

There are four different business plans presented:

Retail
> Will Bullas Store, Inc.--a retail specialty store that sells exclusive products such as clothing, mugs, cards, towels, etc., with licensed designs by the artist, Will Bullas.

Service
> Siempre Envisions--a home-based design graphic and technical documentation business.

Manufacturing
> East Side Plating Company--a company that offers a unique plating service for copper, nickel, and chrome from small; to medium-sized metal pieces.

Product
> Sweet Alternatives--a retail cookie shop that produces and sells low-fat desserts that are satisfying, but low in fat and cholesterol.

After you locate the business plan that is similar to your business, use this sample to help you design your business plan. Remember to customize the information you include in your plan while following the suggested outline, subtitles and questions listed in The Entrepreneur's Planning Handbook. This book provides one of the clearest, easiest and most professional approaches to writing a business plan.

The basic models in these sample business plans should be modified to reflect your business. They offer examples and guidance on customizing your business plan. But these plans are not perfect. Each plan is introduced by a business plan critique highlighting the strengths and weaknesses of each plan. These critiques explain how each strength enhances the business plan and how each weakness might negatively affect the business plan. Do not let the business plans that were written on computers with sophisticated software programs discourage you from preparing yours. These business plans were selected to show you various formats and designs that can be designed with today's computer technology.

The sample business plans appear in this book back to back. However when writing your plan only put text on the right page - never write your plan using both sides of the page. Also, to save space and because of proprietary information, only the Table of Contents for the Appendix is included for each business plan.

Remember, the value of writing a business plan comes from your going through the experience of researching, investigating, preparing, and designing the critical information required for the planning process that is essential to make your business successful. Today, the more entrepreneurs who use available computer technology to help them communicate and write their planning documents, the higher their chances for success.

Carefully review the business plan critique that appears before each selected business plan. Examine the strengths and weaknesses of each plan, and learn from these critiques. They are identical to the ones you will receive in the FastTrac program after you have completed your business plan.

Premier FastTrac's <u>Sample Business Plans</u> is a valuable tool for you to enhance your business planning skills and turn out winning business plans.

We want to thank the following entrepreneurs, students, and FastTrac graduates who allowed us to use their business plans as samples for this book:

SWEET ALTERNATIVES

Business Plan Written by:
> Deborah Clark
> Jennifer Scott
> Julie Davis
> Craig Kwitoski

WILL BULLAS INCORPORATED

Business Plan Written by:
> Erin Rosenwald

SIEMPRE ENVISIONS

Business Plan Written by:
> Catherine Hawthorne

EAST SIDE PLATING COMPANY

Business Plan Written by:
> Jack P. Osten

Their business plans have already and will continue to help strengthen the business planning skills of our FastTrac graduates. The authors sincerely thank them for their contributions to enhancing the skills of entrepreneurs.

CHAPTER 1
SWEET ALTERNATIVES

Written by:

    Deborah Clark
    Jennifer Scott
    Julie Davis
    Craig Kwitoski

Computer hardware:

    Apple Macintosh

Computer software:

    Microsoft Word, Microsoft Excel, Microsoft Draw

Printing:

    Kinko's Copies

Book used to write business plan:

    <u>The Entrepreneur's Planning Handbook</u>

Overview

The Entrepreneurship Program, School of Business Administration at the University of Southern California, is one of the oldest entrepreneurship programs in the United States. It was started in 1972. The original entrepreneurship program consisted of only an MBA program. It was expanded in 1981 to include an undergraduate program in entrepreneurship education. School of Business undergraduate students, for their senior option, can choose to obtain an emphasis in entrepreneurship by completing four entrepreneurship courses, each 4 hours, totaling 16 hours of college credit.

The program is taught in a lock-step format, which requires students to take all four courses with the same group of students. Students cannot opt to take one or two of the courses, but must complete all the courses in their required sequence. Assigned projects in the entrepreneurship courses include both a group business plan, during the fall semester, and an individual business plan, during the spring semester.

The reason for requiring students to write two business plans is that the group plan teaches students to work with each other. Thus it strengthens their communication and networking skills while they learn format and writing skills for developing a business plan. Completing an individual business plan, during the spring semester, is their second attempt at preparing a business plan. It allows them to concentrate on researching and preparing the critical information that should be included in the business plan.

The Sweet Alternative business plan was chosen from student group business plans written during the fall semester. This business plan, written by the above group of students, was selected to be included in this book because of the eye-appealing presentation in both format and writing style. This business plan also closely followed the suggested format and subtitles found in <u>The Entrepreneur's Business Planning Handbook</u>. The business plan critique points out that the main weakness is missing information from some sections, which results in incomplete sections.

The founders of Premier FastTrac II entrepreneurial training programs realize that many FastTrac participants will not spend the hours nor have the resources to prepare this type of business plan. However, you will notice how a computer makes it possible to display information and create graphics in various attractive formats. This enhances the overall look of the business plan.

If your business plan is intended to raise money, remember that the better the visual presentation, the better chance you have of raising the amount of capital you have targeted. Potential investors are impressed by a professionally prepared and eye-appealing business plan.

Carefully read all the comments included in the Business Plan Critique and learn from the strengths and weakness of this plan.

The authors of <u>The Entrepreneur's Business Plan Handbook</u> want to thank Debbie, Jennie, Julie and Craig for letting us discuss their plan and using it as an example for FastTracers. At the present time, the business is still in the planning stage. In order not to disclose proprietary information, the Appendix was deleted since it contained trade secret recipes, etc.

BUSINESS PLAN CRITIQUE

Name: Sweet Alternatives

I. Overall Appearance and Format

The entrepreneurs rearranged the suggested format for their business plan so that the last section is the financial plan. This is not necessarily wrong and has some merit since the financial section is the summation of the plan. However, this is only one of a few sections that should be rearranged, as noted later.

The length is approximately 60 pages, which is appropriate for this business plan. There is excellent use of charts, graphs, pictures, etc. The header on each page is attractive. It keeps the reader focused on the product and key elements of the plan. The exhibits are properly identified in the Appendix, including footnotes.

II. Cover Page

Strength:

This page catches the reader's attention with the name of the company and an attractive picture of product; i.e., cookies.

Weakness:

It fails to list the contact person's name, address and telephone number.

III. Table of Contents

It includes all the major sections along with the page numbers.

IV. Executive Summary

Strength:

It is written in letter form and addressed to the reader of the plan. This letter highlights all the key areas of the plan so the reader gets an overview of the business.

BUSINESS PLAN CRITIQUE

V. Management and Organization

Strength:

There is an excellent listing of the contracts and agreements that will be used in the business. Much of the information in this section is listed in bullet form, which makes it easy to read. It also includes all the important information for this section.

Weakness:

Advisory Council

This section includes members of the infrastructure, who should be listed under a separate subheading. When both are included together, it is confusing to the reader. It is difficult to identify who is a member of the infrastructure and who is on the advisory council.

VI. Product/Service

Strength:

Purpose of the Product

There is a good explanation of the product without using meaningless adjectives. It is to the point and is easy to understand.

Trademarks, Patents, Copyrights

The plan includes all proprietary rights, and if properly protected, could add great value to the company now and in the future.

Weakness:

Production

A subcontractor to make cookie dough has not been secured. This takes credibility away from the plan and leaves doubt with the reader whether these recipes could be mass-produced. This section indicates that since the company has not located a subcontractor, it will not be able to specify a true cost for the product. This invalidates the financial projections contained in the plan.

BUSINESS PLAN CRITIQUE

VII. Marketing Plan

Strength:

Market Niche

There is good use of graphics and charts.

Competitive Matrix Chart

It is attractive and easy to read and includes all the necessary information.

Customer Profile

The plan uses charts, which makes it easier for the reader to read and understand.

Advertising and Promotion

This subhead includes press releases, identifies talk shows, and describes promotions that will be scheduled on radio stations and in newspapers.

Weakness:

Packaging and Labeling

This subhead should have included an example of the package and identified a manufacturer so the reader knows that the packaging costs have been properly researched.

Gross margin on products

The gross margin is incorrect. It should be:
total sales − cost of goods sold = gross margin
299,066 − 60,984 = 238,082
sales divided by gross margin = gross margin percentage
238,082 / 299,066 = 79%

BUSINESS PLAN CRITIQUE

VIII. Financial Plan

Strength:

<u>Assumptions</u>

Assumptions are complete and include good detail. The assumption numbers correspond with the Chart of Accounts contained in the Cash Flow. This allows the reader to determine how each expense entry was calculated by being able to refer back to the cash flow assumptions.

Weakness:

Some expenses will parallel sales volume; i.e. the higher the volume, the higher the expenses such as salaries, telephone, supplies and so forth. Readers do no like to see straight-line projections where expenses are identical every month, regardless of the volume, unless it is a fixed expense. Straight lining expenses indicates that the entrepreneurs do not have a good understanding of how expenses vary with sales volume.

IX. Operating System

Strength:

The charts and product flow chart are excellent examples of how to incorporate a flow chart. The entire section contains good details and gives the reader confidence that the management team knows how the business will operate.

X. Growth Plan

Strength:

This section includes charts, which makes it easier to read and understand

XI. Appendix

<u>Note:</u>

Only the cover page of the Appendix has been included because of the length of the entire Appendix, and trade secrets contained in this section..

**Business Plan
November 29, 1993**

Deborah Clark, CEO
Sweet Alternatives
2610 Portland, Suite 206
Los Angeles, CA 90007

November 29, 1993

Dear Mack:

Sweet Alternatives is a retail cookie shop located on 3rd Street Promenade in the Santa Monica Bayside District. It was established to offer the health conscious consumer a dessert that is satisfying, yet low in fat and cholesterol. The company is confident that the current health awareness trend will continue to grow within the next several years as consumers look toward a healthier lifestyle. *Sweet Alternatives* has devised recipes that contain no added fat and use all natural substitutes such as apples, bananas, prune puree and non-fat dairy products.

United States consumer cookie and cracker expenditures grew three percent from $8.3 million in 1992 to $8.6 million in 1993. Currently, fat-free cookies hold a nine percent share of the cookie and cracker market and are expected to grow more than two percent annually for the next five years. This growth is attributed to the increase in health awareness by young professionals, baby boomers and senior citizens. Using these statistics, *Sweet Alternatives* expects revenues of $13 thousand in its first month of operations.

Sweet Alternatives will be an S-corporation with Deborah Clark as the Chief Executive Officer, Craig Kwitoski as the Chief Financial Officer, Jennie Scott as the Chief Operations Officer, and Julie Davis as the Executive Vice-President: Sales and Marketing. Every member of the management team possesses the skills needed to fulfill the responsibilities of their prospective position.

The Advisory Council consists of Bill Sanderson, President of Popcorn Palace and Candy Emporium, Ken Davis, President of Quality Tune-up, Dan Neynenues, President of Gold Coast Catering and Karen Hall, Personal Nutritionist. Our infrastructure includes Janet Garner, independent CPA and Allen Wiener, corporate attorney.

The marketing plan will consist of heavy penetration the first two months of operation followed by an intense advertising campaign. Advertising will increase during holiday months. *Sweet Alternatives* will obtain publicity by sending press releases prior to the grand opening. In addition, the company will also use a *Sweet Alternatives* Cookie Cart located directly on the Promenade to offer free samples to our customers. This will help introduce our product to the foot traffic on 3rd Street who may not be aware of our newly established cookie shop.

Sweet Alternatives direct competitors are cookie and snack retailers located in the Bayside District. These include Mrs. Field's, Lisa's Bakery, ACME Bakery and Humphrey's Yogurt. Mrs. Field's main strength is its international name recognition for quality baked goods. Lisa's bakery and ACME bakery claim to have great tasting desserts. However, their hidden locations are their major weakness. Although Humphrey's Yogurt has an excellent location, its main downfall is its wide selection of products which deters from its specialty of custom made yogurt.

Each of the directors own 25 percent of the company and have invested $31,250. This initial investment of $125,000 is forecast to be recovered within 3.5 years and will be paid back to investors through stock.

Sincerely,

Deborah L. Clark,
Chief Executive Officer,
Sweet Alternatives

TABLE OF CONTENTS

Management and Organization

Product / Service Plan

Marketing Plan

Operating System

Growth Plan

Financial Plan

APPENDIX

Management
&
Organization

MANAGEMENT AND ORGANIZATION

Chief Executive Officer

Deborah Clark is leading *Sweet Alternatives* with over eight years leadership and managerial experience in all different aspects of business. Her responsibilities as a student coordinator for the University and Alumni Events have included coordinating events, organizing invitations, setting event budgets, and planning catering specifications. She has also lead her chapter house as Vice President: Chapter Programming. She supervises a board of ten officers and leads a chapter of over 100 women. Working as a fashion and makeup consultant at her mother's clothing business for over four years has provided her with an extensive background in customer service and entrepreneurship. Deborah has a grasp of the effort needed to make *Sweet Alternatives* a success. Currently attending the University of Southern California, Ms. Clark is pursuing her B.S. in Business Administration with an emphasis in entrepreneur.

Responsibilities

The Chief Executive Officer(CEO) is responsible for strategic issues, external relations, and overall corporate governance. By definition the CEO's role is to synthesize, from internal and external sources, the companies long term goals and objectives, which become, in their composite form, the company's vision. The CEO must also play a major role in supporting that vision both by example and by internally communicating it's nature and importance. At *Sweet Alternatives*, the CEO will ensure that our corporation continues to meet both the employee's and the customer's needs. When the CEO feels that a different route is needed to increase the profit of the company, she will discuss the problem with her executive team, and come to a decision to keep sales high as well as employees and customers happy.

Chief Financial Officer

Craig M. Kwitoski will manage the finances of *Sweet Alternatives*. He has gained valuable knowledge of money management from his experience at Wells Fargo and Alex Brown, and Sons. At each of these positions, not only was he responsible for the financial aspects of the business; cash flows, expense reports, profit reports and budgets, he was also involved in advertising, telemarketing and public relations. His vast experience in all areas of business will prove to be a valuable asset to *Sweet Alternatives'* daily financial operations.

Responsibilities

The role of the Chief Financial Officer(CFO) is to control all financial operations of a corporation. The CFO oversees all accounts receivable, accounts payable, employee payroll and inventory. The CFO provides a corporation with an organized vision of the companies financial situation. Also, the CFO forms the companies cash flows, balance sheets, and income statements. These figures show the companies profits and losses, and forecasts the growth and success of the business.

Chief Operations Officer

Jennie Scott brings her experience as a sales representative and customer service representative to *Sweet Alternatives*. Her extensive background with product control makes her the best choice for the job. She has worked in many different retail stores which gave her the experience needed to know what the consumer needs and wants in a product. Currently, she is developing the secret recipes for all of the working prototypes for *Sweet Alternatives*. Ms. Scott will be the mover and shaker of the product and internal controls. Ms. Scott will be able to foresee what is needed in the future to improve current programs. She will monitor all operations and see that they are completed efficiently and profitably.

Responsibilities

Chief Operations Officer(COO) has the general responsibility to oversee daily operations of *Sweet Alternatives*. COO must order all of the inventory needed to make the products and see that they are made correctly with the right ingredients. She will oversee the production of the product to ensure that they are being produced correctly and in accordance with health department regulations.

Executive VP: Sales/Marketing

Julie Davis serves as the head of the marketing efforts for *Sweet Alternatives*. Her experience ranges from Sales Associate and Personal Shopper at Nordstrom to a Sales Representative for Nike. She is currently receiving her B.S. at the University of Southern California with an emphasis in entrepreneur. Before joining the entrepreneur program, Ms. Davis focused her studies in marketing. She has been a part of a marketing team where she created and developed the entire marketing plan for a made-up product. She is also involved with the American Advertising Federation of America.

Responsibilities

The Executive VP: Sales/Marketing is responsible for determining all marketing strategies, pricing, sales, and product marketing. This position also designs and oversees the advertising strategy which includes investigating the target market, the competition and the industry. She will determine which methods of market penetration will be most effective during the introductory phase of the product, and continue to collect sales data to improve the product and the company. The ultimate goal of the Executive VP: Sales/Marketing is to offer the public a quality product that is affordable as well as beneficial to its consumer. There will be continuous follow-up methods to observe the consumers response so that *Sweet Alternatives* can cater to its clientele in the most profitable manner.

See Appendix Exhibit B-2 & C-8

MANAGEMENT ORGANIZATION CHART
1st year

- **Deborah L. Clark** — President & CEO
  - **Jennie Scott** — COO
  - **Julie K. Davis** — Vice President: Sales & Marketing
    - **Sales Manager**
      - Staff
      - Staff
  - **Craig Kwitowski** — CFO
    - Accountant

Board of Directors

Director	Investment	%
Deborah Clark, Chairman of the Board	$31,250	25%
Craig Kwitoski, Secretary/Treasurer	$31,250	25%
Jennie Scott, Director	$31,250	25%
Julie Davis, Director	$31,250	25%

Advisory Council/Infrastructure

	Corporation	Qualifications
Bill Sanderson, President/COB	Popcorn Palace & Candy Emporium (714)547-3681	• Experience in the snack food industry • Familiar with target market • Has a large network of contacts within the industry

Karen Hall, R.D.,C.D.E. Nutritionist	Nutrition Counseling Services 2121 W. Magnolia Burbank, CA 91506 (818)841-9800	• Registered Dietitian
		• Certified Diabetes Educator
		• Specializes in:
		    Nutrition
		    Weight control
		    Clinical Diets

Ken Davis, President/COB	Quality Tune-up 16110 Matillja Drive Los Gatos, CA 95030 (415)866-9332	• Entrepreneur • Familiar with customer service • Knowledge of business trends
Dan Neynenues, President, Owner	Gold Coast Catering 12521 Barranca Parkway Irvine, CA 92716 (714)846-4989	• Knowledge of food industry • Knowledge of product • Knowledge of operations
Janet Garner, CPA	Self Employed 874 N. Red Robin Blvd. Orange, CA 92669 (714)633-8788	• MBA, Drake University • CPA over 20 years • Specializes in small business startups
Allen Wiener, Corporate Attorney	Bosley & Wiener Associates 333 Michelson Drive Irvine, CA 92714 (714)559-3220	• Attorney over 20 years • Specializes in small businesses

Contracts and Agreements

S-Corporation

- Business License Agreement
- Form SS-4: Federal Employer Identification Number
- Form DE-1: State Employer Number
- Form 1120S: Federal S-Corp. Income Tax Return
- Form 100S: State S-Corp. Income Tax Return
- Form 8109-B: Federal Payroll & Corporate Tax Deposit
- Form DE-3M: State Payroll Tax Deposit
- Form 941: Federal Quarterly Payroll Tax Return
- Form 940: Federal Annual Unemployment Tax Return
- Form DE-3DP: State Quarterly Payroll Tax Return

Employment

- Form W-4
- Form W-2: Wage Statement for Employees
- Employee Non-compete Agreement (Specific Radius)
- Employee Secrecy Agreement
- Employee Confidentiality Agreement
- Equal Opportunity Agreement

Intellectual

- Non-disclosure/Non-compete Agreement during all property stages of production, growth and dismissal
- Confidentiality Disclosure Agreement
- Trademark Application

See Appendix Exhibit A-1 through A-8 & A-9 through A-19

Insurance Plan

Company	Prudential Insurance 625 Fair Oaks South Pasadena, CA (818)799-2053
Contact	Christian Griffee
Policy	$100,000 Buy/Sell Agreement
Premium	$160/year/person

Compensation Packages

Director	Salary	Benefits
Deborah Clark	$24,999	Full Health Coverage
Craig Kwitoski	$24,999	Full Health Coverage
Jennie Scott	$24,999	Full Health Coverage
Julie Davis	$24,999	Full Health Coverage

Product / Service Plan

PRODUCT & SERVICE PLAN

Purpose of the Product

The purpose of *Sweet Alternatives* is to provide a low-fat snack substitute to health conscious consumers of all age groups. With the rapid growth of health awareness in Southern California and the increase in production of fat-free cookies by large snack food manufacturers, *Sweet Alternatives* will take the low-fat cookie craze out of the grocery store and into shopping mall. Our product will offer consumers a quick dessert food to satisfy their sweet tooth without the fat.

Unique Features

<u>Product</u>

- made with the following natural low-fat substitutes: apples, bananas, prune puree, and non-fat dairy products

- sold for $1.00/item

- produced from scratch by an outside manufacturer

- developed and refined by gourmet cookie chefs and qualified nutritionists

- produced approximately 91% fat-free with 60 calories

- produced to be moist, light, and full of rich flavor

Stage of Development

After testing various forms of fat substitutes, *Sweet Alternatives* has developed seven different working prototypes. As a result of our research and development efforts, *Sweet Alternatives* will be using the following ingredients as fat substitutes:

- apple sauce
- dried plum puree
- non-fat yogurt
- low fat cottage cheese
- bananas

The history of our product development began with research. After consulting articles, statistics, bakeries and nutritionists, we compiled a list of over twenty commonly used fat replacers. We cross referenced this list with statistics that revealed that some of the synthetic fat substitutes were not as healthy as previously thought. We then narrowed our list down to only natural substitutes.

The next step was to use these natural ingredients as substitutes in numerous cookie and brownie recipes. Through trial and error, and the guidance of our nutritionist, we continued to narrow our list even further. Our final decision was based on the texture, flavor, consistency, and presentation of our products.

See Appendix Exhibit C-1

Future Research and Development

Sweet Alternatives is a young corporation. We realize competing with large cookie manufacturers will be difficult and costly. However, through our innovative research and development methods, we feel that we can alleviate this problem:

Method	Cost	Additional Employees Required
Obtain a current fat substitute information database	$0.00	none
Gain a membership in the Calorie Control Council, etc.	$200.00	none
Subscribe to Bakers News and other diet and health magazines.	Subscription fees	none
Hold a fat-free baking competition	$2,000 per year plus percentage of that product sold for 1 year.	none
Create a Snack Development Program	Culinary school tuition, supplies, consultant fees	none

Benefits

These new methods will provide a continuous update of the current fat substitutes and industry changes. *Sweet Alternatives* will network our product through the trade association to get a feel for the competition and the strength of our position in the industry. These methods will also provide a very low cost way to keep up with the low-fat craze without additional employee labor. The baking competition is particularly unique. *Sweet Alternatives* will hold a recipe competition at local baking schools for the best low-fat cookie produced. The winner will receive a prize of $500 plus 1 percent of sales of that cookie sold for one year. Also, the cookie will be named after the winner for one year of production. Our Snack Development Program allows the owners to become involved in the production of our product. Each *Sweet Alternatives* owner will enroll in culinary school to learn the art of baking. This will allow the management team to continue experimenting with new products as well as become aware of the baking trade. We feel it is important for every owner to understand the process of baking low-fat desserts.

Trademarks, Patents, Copyrights, Licenses, Royalties

Trademark
Our trademark will consist of the name *Sweet Alternatives* written in white script, on a black scroll, accompanied by a group of chocolate chip cookies.

Trade Secret
Sweet Alternatives will maintain the confidentiality of our recipe through a strict internal control system. Every owner, employee, baker, and perspective investor will sign a non-disclosure, non-compete agreement. This will prevent any false reproduction of our product.

Copyright
In the event we publish our recipes, we will obtain the proper copyright protection.

See Appendix Exhibit A-1 through A-5

Government Approvals
Sweet Alternatives will abide by all regulations set by the Health Department.

See Appendix Exhibit A-20 through A-22

Product Limitation

- After baking, shelf life is limited to one day
- Frozen dough has a shelf life of one month
- Dairy products have a shelf life of one week
- Health Department rules and regulations
- No cookie on display will be sold after 2 hours

See Appendix Exhibit A-20 through A-22

Product Liability

- Food Poisoning

- Allergic Reactions to products

    See Appendix Exhibit A-23

Spin-offs

- Low-fat ice cream cookie sandwiches

- Mini Dough Bites

- Low-fat/Non-fat Muffins

- Dough Bite Bon-Bons

    See Appendix Exhibit C-3

Production

All *Sweet Alternatives* cookies and brownies will be manufactured by an outside supplier, yet to be determined.

Environmental Factors

Packaging Problem
Many of the packaging products are produced using cloro floro carbons (CFC's).

Packaging Solution
Sweet Alternatives will use only recycled paper products. We will not support any packaging that produces CFC's during production.

Production Problem
An abundance of paper products are used for supplies and packaging

Production Solution
Sweet Alternatives will set up a controlled recycling system. Half of our paper will be recycled by the Los Angeles Recycling Center. The other half will be given to local community schools for paper drives.

Gas Problem
Gases used in our baking and freezing units have the possibility to leak into the environment.

Gas Solution
Sweet Alternatives will develop a control system responsible for monitoring these units. This is still being researched to find the most effective method.

Marketing
Plan

MARKETING PLAN

Industry Profile (Source: <u>U.S. Industrial Outlook 1993</u>- Dept. of Commerce)

Current size
According to the U.S. Department of Commerce, the value of total cookies sold within the snack food industry was $8.6 billion in 1993 and the total consumption of cookies was 3.2 billion pounds in 1992.

Growth potential
The health and fitness craze has continued to influence the consumption of low-fat foods. The popularity of low-fat, cholesterol free cookie's and cracker's has grown as well, and is predicted to influence the profits of the entire industry over the next few years. Although consumers include all age groups, customers between the ages of 35-54 show the highest percentage of consumption. The growing concern about health within this age group will help to make the health snack trend stronger. All bakery goods are predicted to rise from 1.5-2 percent annually from 1993-1997. However, the fastest growth will be cookies and crackers at 2 percent annually.

Geographic locations
Sweet Alternatives chose to open their initial shop in the Santa Monica Bayside District due to the overwhelming number of health conscious consumers in that area. Through our research we have found that the healthy eating trend is extremely popular with the residents of Southern California.

Industry trends
Price, convenience, and health concerns will be shaping the snack food industry over the next three years. Although there were increases in the consumption of sweet baked goods in 1987, this growth slowed in 1992. Consumers began to look for snack foods and breakfast foods that were lower in fat and calories. Low-fat cookie varieties are the wave of the future.

See Appendix Exhibit C-8

Seasonality Factors
Research has shown cookie sales to reach their highest point in December during the holiday season. Polls also show that sales increase during the winter months. These statistics are based on the assumption that consumers are searching for a warm snack to satisfy their sweet tooth during the colder months. In contrast, statistics show that sales are steady during the summer months.

Profit Characteristics
The snack food industry has a profit margin of 78 percent. This holds true within the sub-industry of cookie and crackers as well. This industry is characterized by:

- costs of goods sold equals approximately 22% of sales.

- production of frozen and fresh bakery items

- importance of fat, cholesterol and calorie percentage within each product

See Appendix Exhibit C-8

Distribution Networks
- Food brokers

- Grocery stores

- Dessert manufacturers

- Bakeries

- Retail snack stores

Industry Competition (Source: Milling and Baking News 10-12-93 / 4-13-93)

Manufactures	Price	Quality	Promotion	Service
Nabisco: Chips Ahoy Fig Newtons Oreo's Snackwells	$1.99-$2.50	• Good - Avg. • Many brands are processed • Fat-free products are growing in popularity	• Advertising • Promotion • Coupons • Public Service	• Sold through grocers and mini markets
Private Labels: Sam's Choice Master Choice President's Choice	$1.50-$2.50	• Good - Fair • Popular • Fresher than other competition	• Advertising • Promotion • Coupons • Public Service	• Sold through grocers and mini markets
Bakeries/Retail Stores	$.95 and up	• Excellent - Good • Baked fresh daily • No preservatives • More popular	• Fliers, coupons, mailings • Press Releases	• Personal • Convenient • Meets desires of consumers

See Marketing Plan: Competitive Matrix Chart for more detailed competition

Competition Profile

Operations

- *Sweet Alternatives* uses a manufacturer to produce it's product. This provides inexpensive, efficient, fast delivery of our product to our consumer.

- *Sweet Alternatives* offers a fast food service for the consumer who wants a quick, convenient snack.

- *Sweet Alternatives* offers an unlimited amount of cookies and brownies to our customer. They will always be delivered fresh and warm to ensure our customer is satisfied with our product.

Management

- The *Sweet Alternatives* employees will work as part of a management team. We will take the time to hire experienced, older employees so that they may be involved in decision making.

- Although *Sweet Alternatives* is still a young company, the management team is working on developing a positive training program so that all employees can benefit from their *Sweet Alternatives* experience.

Product

- *Sweet Alternatives*' products are: low-fat, cholesterol free and all natural

- Our variety of products offer a healthy alternative to satisfy our consumer's sweet tooth

Price

- All products will be $1.00 regardless of the type of cookie, brownie or beverage. This price is slightly higher than many of our cookie competitors. However, research has shown that health conscious consumers are willing to pay more for healthier products.

See Appendix Exhibit C-4

Service

- *Sweet Alternatives* will offer friendly, fast service to our consumer

- A "Customer 1st" attitude will be practiced by all *Sweet Alternatives* employees

- Our training program will provide:
    Education on our product
    Education on the Snack Food Industry
    Education on health department rules/regulations
    Education on customer service

Market Niche Opportunities

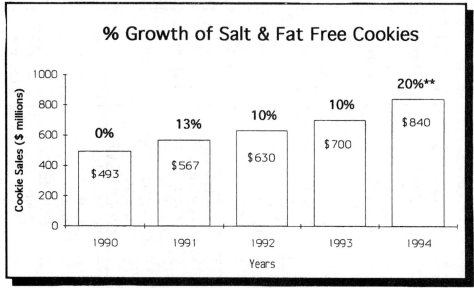

** Predicted growth and cookie sales for 1994

- The recent increase in fat-free substitutes is attributed to the growing popularity of these products with baby boomers, senior citizens, and parents.

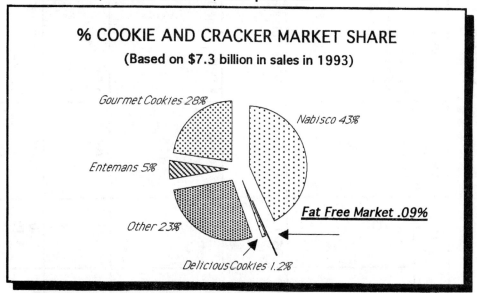

- Fat-free cookies currently hold .09% of the entire cookie market share as shown above. This provides an incredible opportunity for *Sweet Alternatives* to jump into the snack food industry with low-fat products.

COMPETITIVE MATRIX CHART

	Price $	Production/ Quality	Unique Features	Distribution System	Marketing/ Location	Geographic Location	Strengths/ Weaknesses
Sweet Alternatives	1.00	Excellent	• Low-fat • No Cholesterol • Natural Products	Retail	• Mailers • Fliers • Coupons • Sample cart **Location:** Third St. Promenade, Santa Monica	Santa Monica Bayside District	**Strengths:** • Healthy snacks • Fast Service • Location **Weaknesses:** • Young • Unknown • New product
Mrs. Fields	.95-1.30	Excellent	• Incredible taste	Wholesale/ Retail	• No advertising **Location:** Malls	International	**Strengths:** • Internationally known • Excellent quality
Lisa's	.95	Good	• Delivery baskets	Wholesale/ Retail	• Ads in local newspapers • Fliers • Mailers **Location:** Third St. Promenade alley	Santa Monica Bayside District	**Strengths:** • Offers many products **Weaknesses:** • Location
ACME	.95	Great	None	Retail	No Advertising **Location:** Third St. Promenade	Santa Monica Bayside District	**Strengths:** • Location **Weaknesses:** • Winter months
Humphrey's Yogurt	1.50-3.19	Good	• Custom mixed yogurt	Retail	• Fliers **Location:** Third St. Promenade, Open malls	Southern California	**Strengths** • Location • Custom product **Weaknesses:** • Too many products

Customer Profile

AGE	• Senior Citizens: 65 plus • Young Professionals: 30-40 • College Students: 18-25 • Parents of young children • Baby Boomers
SEX	• Male and Female
PROFESSION	• Students • Teachers • Lawyers • Accountants • Young Business Men/Women • Health Professionals • Athletes
INCOME	$20,000 plus
GEOGRAPHIC	Southern California
SOCIAL CLASS	Middle-Upper Class
LIFE STYLE	• Healthy • Active • Physically Fit • Wealthy • Social
PERSONALITY	• Aware of health trends • Aware of the benefits of living a healthy lifestyle

Benefits of *Sweet Alternatives*
- Low-fat, cholesterol free, all natural products
- Quick, convenient, friendly service
- Education of health trends and healthy eating
- Renewed confidence in eating habits

Survey Results
The survey revealed that *Sweet Alternatives* cookies and brownies will satisfy the consumers needs for a snack food with less fat, cholesterol, and calories.

Student/Young Professional Results
- Excited about product
- Would purchase our product over competitor
- Ate the whole batch
- Could not believe the quality and taste
- Melted in mouth
- Concerned that the prototype was not really 91% fat free

Professional/Senior Citizens' Results
- Excited about product
- Could not wait to try another one of our products
- Would buy future products if taste was good
- Enjoyed the taste and texture, and wanted the recipe
- Could not believe they were 91% fat free

See Appendix Exhibit C-5 & C-6

Target Market Profile

Market Niche

The inspiration behind *Sweet Alternatives* was the fact that, as college students, we were in search of a healthy dessert low in fat and cholesterol. Through our research we found that there was a demand for a healthy snack alternative that satisfied the consumer's sweet tooth and still tasted good. *Sweet Alternatives* will take advantage of this demand and enter the snack industry with our low-fat, no cholesterol products.

Target Market

1. Foot traffic on Third Street Promenade
   20,000 customers per weekend

   Cost: $500/cookie cart on the promenade
   $210/week for fliers, coupons

2. Health Conscious Consumer
   Cost: $10,600/year on Advertising/Marketing

Market Penetration

Distribution Channels

- *Sweet Alternatives* will use it's retail store to distribute it's product to the consumers

- As part of our Marketing Plan, we will also use a *Sweet Alternatives* Cookie Cart to offer the foot traffic on the promenade samples of our product. This will entice the consumer to visit our store and buy more products.

Direct Sales Force

CORPORATE STAFF
$20,000/year

CEO	-Deborah Clark
CFO	-Craig Kwitoski
COO	-Jennie Scott
VP Marketing	-Julie Davis

COOKIE SALES ASSOCIATES
Full-time: $8/hour
Part-time: $8/hour

Full-time: 1
Part-time: 2

Each sales associate receives:
- 25% Discount on all products
- Free cookies at end of the day
- Promotional Contest Rewards
- Education of product & industry
- Training in customer service

Direct Mail

Mailer	Mailing List Resources	Cost	Schedule	Response Rate
Grand Opening Brochures	• Health Clubs • Health Magazines • Local Businesses • College Campuses	1000K @ .23/copy	June & July	1-2 weeks after mail date
Holiday/Monthly Brochures	• Health Clubs • Health Magazines • Local Businesses • College Campuses	1000K @ .23/copy	Holidays	1-2 weeks after mail date

See Appendix Exhibit C-7

Advertising and Promotion
Press releases
- L.A. Times
- Santa Monica News
- Wall Street Journal
- Daily News
- Milling and Baking News
- Shape Magazine
- Health and Fitness Magazine

Sweet Alternatives will send four press releases to each periodical describing our product and service during our Grand Opening month. Future press releases will be sent to introduce new products and company developments.

Talk Shows and Radio
- Live: with Regis & Kathy Lee
- Good Morning America
- Good Day L.A.
- KIIS F.M.
- 98.7 KSTR F.M.

Sweet Alternatives will introduce our product to each of these broadcasts with an informational letter. We will follow our introductory letter with a batch of cookies and brownies accompanied by a collection of statistics about our product and current health trends. A follow up phone call will be made by the management team to find out if the media is receptive.

Packaging and Labeling

Sweet Alternatives will package single orders in paper bags labeled with the *Sweet Alternatives* trademark. Orders consisting of one-half a dozen or more can be purchased in a decorative cookie tin.

Service and Warranties

Sweet Alternatives provides a "Satisfaction Guarantee" on all products. If a customer is not satisfied with our cookies or brownies they will be invited to return the uneaten portion of their snack to try another item. If they are still not satisfied, their money will be returned with a coupon for a free cookie.

Future Markets

MARKET	SIZE	PENETRATION	COST
College Campuses	USC UCLA Pepperdine LMU	• Sell product in bookstore/cafe • Distribute fliers and coupons • Offer free samples	• Distributing • Packaging • Advertising
Health Club Snack Bars	Family Fitness Bally's Health Club Sports Club L.A.	• Sell in snack bars • Distribute info-fliers and coupons • Offer nutrition workshops • Offer free samples	• Distributing • Packaging • Advertising
Coffee Houses	Local, Bayside Coffee Houses	• Distribute info-fliers and coupons • Offer free coffee with cookie/brownie of the day	• Distributing • Packaging • Advertising

Pricing Profile

MENU
($1 EACH ITEM)

THE HEALTHY CHIP
CINNAMON OATMEAL
CHERRY OATMEAL CHEW
GINGER CINNAMON CRISP
GRANOLA YOGURT CHIP
CLASSIC SUGAR COOKIE
DOUBLE DUTCH DELITE
APPLE SPICE SQUARES
BROWNIE BITES

BEVERAGES
Bottled water, soda, juice, milk
Coffee
Cappuccino/Double
Espresso/Double
Cafe latte
Cafe au lait
Cafe mocha
Hot chocolate
Apple cider

Summer Promotional Sales
- Buy two cookies, get one free
- Buy three cookies, get one free cappuccino
- Wednesday coffee specials: $.50

Season Promotional Sales
- December: Filled holiday cookie tins ($9.95)
- February: One dozen cookies in a heart tin ($9.95)

Industry Pricing Policies

The average industry price for a cookie is $.95. Although *Sweet Alternatives* is slightly higher, $1.00/cookie, research has shown that health conscious consumers are willing to pay more for all natural ingredients.

Pricing all of our products at $1.00/item will differentiate *Sweet Alternatives* from the competition.

See Appendix Exhibit C-4

Gross Margin on Products

Sweet Alternatives will have a 4.91 percent gross margin on products. This figure was arrived at by taking Total Sales/COGS, $299,066/$60,984.

Operating System

OPERATING SYSTEM

Administrative Policies, Procedures and Controls

Receiving Orders

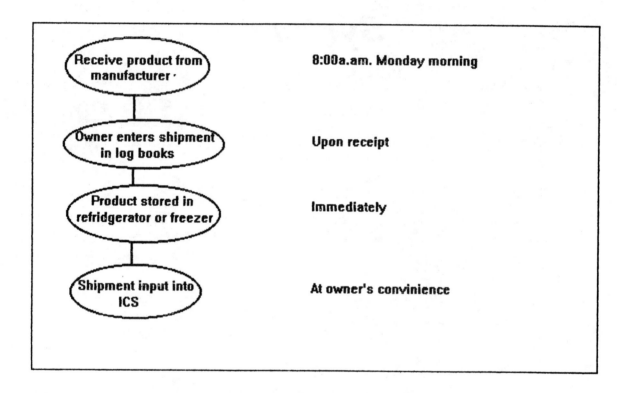

Our orders will consist of batches of cookie dough and brownie mix. They will be delivered from our manufacturer, which is to be determined at a later date, two hours before the store opens Monday morning. The shipment will provide enough batches for the following week. We will have an emergency order if we run out of cookies before the next delivery.

The delivery will be logged in our inventory book upon arrival and then input into our computerized inventory control system. Monday's cookies will be prepared that morning and throughout the day as needed. The remaining batches will be stored in the freezer until taken out to thaw in the refrigerator, the night before baking.

Our individual beverages and coffee will be received monthly through Bravo Coffee Distributor. Coca Cola Company will deliver bottled sodas, water and juices monthly. Bravo Coffee Distributor will deliver their Italian roast coffee, Talantani, as needed by the case. Our daily supply of beverages will be stored in our refrigerators and the coffee in our dry storage facility. Orders will be logged into our inventory book upon arrival and then input into our computerized inventory control system.

Packaging and paper supplies will be received bi-monthly. Two boxes of approximately 8,000 packaging and paper supplies will be delivered every 15 days. The supplies will be logged in our inventory book upon arrival and input into our computerized inventory control system.

Billing Customers

All collections of sales will be made COD. *Sweet Alternatives* will sell each item at a price of $1.00 regardless of the type of cookie, brownie, or beverage.

Paying Suppliers

Sweet Alternatives will pay the following on a net 30 basis:
- Manufacturer of cookie and brownie batches
- Bravo Coffee Distributor
- Coca Cola Company
- Packaging and Paper Supplier
- Phone, Gas, and Electric Companies

Management Schedule

Sweet Alternatives will use cooperative efforts between the four owners to develop a management team that will provide the most efficient and pleasant atmosphere. Our goal is to use each of the owners' expertise to keep ahead of our competition. Therefore, a structured management plan is very essential. The four owners will meet once a week to discuss:

- upcoming sales and promotional tactics
- internal/external problems
- solutions to these problems
- customer service
- new developments within the snack food and fat-free food industry

Also, once a month the entire *Sweet Alternatives* staff will meet to share any frustrations and concerns they have about their responsibilities within the company. This meeting will also be used as a brainstorming session on how *Sweet Alternatives* can increase sales, produce new product lines, and increase awareness of our company and our product. Involving our employees in the development process of our company will increase their knowledge of the company and create a desire for them to be involved in the success of *Sweet Alternatives*.

Employee Training, Promotions and Incentives

Sweet Alternatives will provide our own internal training and education of our product. It is important that each owner and employee represent *Sweet Alternatives* with the essential facts and statistics that separate us from our competitors. Our training program will provide:

- Education on our product and its unique features

- Education on the Snack Food Industry: any new developments on fat substitutes, any new competitors created in the industry, any new information on our target consumer

- Education on new health department rules and regulations

- Education on customer service and how to educate our consumer about our product

- Videos that describe the *Sweet Alternatives* concept

Employee promotions and incentives will focus on making the employee excited to be involved with *Sweet Alternatives*. They will allow the employees to be an active team player with the company's development techniques while enjoying working for our company.

Motivational techniques

- Offer above minimum wage to attract better qualified, older employees

- Create selling contest between employees on promotional and seasonal items

- Hold cookie races for daily left over cookies

- Provide inspirational meetings each month for employee input on how to increase sales and awareness of our company

- Offer employees a 25% discount on all cookies purchased and free drinks while working

- Provide a "Day of Management" to allow staff to manage *Sweet Alternatives*. This will be implemented as *Sweet Alternatives* has more employees.

- Recognize an "Employee of the Month"

- Give holiday parties for all employees

- Allow employees to develop their own low-fat recipes and experiment at *Sweet Alternatives*

- Offer every employee the title of Cookie Sales Associate

Computerized Inventory Control System (ICS)

Our inventory will be controlled through our personalized Inventory Control System(ICS). This system will help keep track of all items coming into and going out of the store in an effective and efficient manner.

Inventory Control System

1. As the inventory is delivered to the store, an owner will log the shipment into our inventory log book. This will provide a hard copy of what has been received into inventory and a record of the date of shipment.

2. Once the inventory has been properly stored, an owner will enter the shipment into our computer. This inventory system is a custom inventory control system created for *Sweet Alternatives*. There will be no extra expense for this system. The system was developed by Jim Clark, and he has allowed *Sweet Alternatives* to use his program at no cost.

   The program allows *Sweet Alternatives* to:
   - record all items received into inventory

   - provide a running total of every item in inventory

   - provide an update at the end of each week and each month to ensure that *Sweet Alternatives* is operating at a profit.

   - monitor each team member's sales through an individual code number. This will help to provide correct percentages of each type of cookie sold by each employee.

3. Once the cookies are ready for sale the transaction will be recorded as follows:

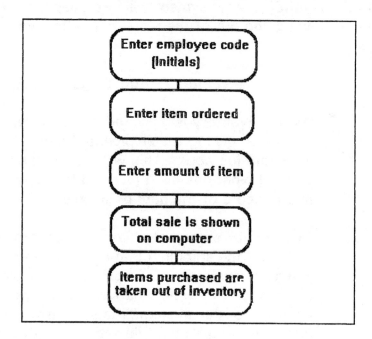

See Appendix Exhibit B-1

Warranties and Returns
Sweet Alternatives provides a "Satisfaction Guarantee" on all products. If a customer is not satisfied with our cookies or brownies, they will be invited to return the uneaten portion of their snack to try another item. If they are still not satisfied, their money will be returned with a coupon for a free cookie.

Company Budgets
All business expenses will be monitored very closely. Our goal is to keep costs low with the optimal return in sales. The following conditions will apply:

Phone
- There will be no personal phone calls, except for emergencies
- Phone calls will be limited to distributors and manufacturers
- We estimate an average expense of $150/month for the phone bill

Supply
- Our strict inventory system will provide a weekly printout to show inventory updates
- Maintenance on fixed supplies will be on an as needed basis to keep our equipment working
- Our supply budget will consist of $3,800/month for packaging, paper and office supplies, and smallwares

Trade Secrets:

Sweet Alternatives will protect its trade secrets through contracts established with the owners and employees. The following contracts will be mandatory before any person or legal entity becomes involved with *Sweet Alternatives*:

Employment

- Employee Non-compete Agreement (Specific Radius)
- Employee Secrecy Agreement
- Employee Confidentiality Agreement

Intellectual

- Non-disclosure/Non-compete Agreement during all Property stages of production, growth and dismissal
- Confidentiality Disclosure Agreement
- Non-disclosure Agreement

See Appendix Exhibit A-1 through A-6

Transaction Documents Needed

- Invoices for all supplies delivered to *Sweet Alternatives* from product manufacturer and suppliers
- Inventory log book
- Weekly/Monthly printout of inventory status
- Receipt for customers
- Deposit forms and bank receipts

Product/Service Flow

```
                    ┌─────────────────────┐
                    │ Produced by manufacturer │
                    └─────────────────────┘
                              │                         Return to
                              ▼                         manufacturer
                    ┌─────────────────────┐
                    │   Delivered to      │
                    │ Sweet Alternatives  │
                    └─────────────────────┘
                              │
                              ▼                          ┌────┐
                    ┌─────────────────────┐              │ No │
                    │ Received by management │──► Satisfactory ├────┤
                    └─────────────────────┘              │ Yes│
                              │                          └────┘
                              ▼
                    ┌─────────────────────┐
                    │ Logged into inventory books │
                    └─────────────────────┘
                              │
                              ▼
                  ┌─────────────────────────────┐
                  │ Weeks supply of cookie dough │
                  │ and brownie mix put into freezer │
                  └─────────────────────────────┘
                        │             │
                        ▼             ▼
           ┌──────────────────┐  ┌──────────────────┐
           │ Days supply put  │  │ Shipment input into ICS │
           │ into refrigerator│  │ by management    │
           └──────────────────┘  └──────────────────┘
                    │
                    ▼
           ┌──────────────────────────┐
           │ Employees scoop cookies or │
           │ cut brownies for baking pan │
           └──────────────────────────┘
                    │
                    ▼
           ┌──────────────────────────┐          ┌────────────────┐
           │ Bake product for 5-10 minutes │      │ Use as samples │
           │ in convection oven       │          └────────────────┘
           └──────────────────────────┘                  ▲
                    │                              ┌────────────────┐
                    ▼                              │ Give to homeless │
           ┌──────────────────────────┐            └────────────────┘
           │ Cool product on cooling rack │──► Satisfactory ┌────┐
           └──────────────────────────┘                     │ No │
                    │                                       │ Yes│
                    ▼                                       └────┘
           ┌──────────────────────────┐
           │ Place cookies and brownies │
           │ in display pans          │
           └──────────────────────────┘
                    │
                    ▼
           ┌──────────────────────────────┐
           │ Transfer cookies and brownies │
           │ to display counter with heat lamps │
           └──────────────────────────────┘
                    │
                    ▼
           ┌──────────────────────────┐        ┌──────────────────┐
           │ Employees sell product   │        │ Customers leave  │
           └──────────────────────────┘        │ satisfied!       │
                    │                          └──────────────────┘
                    ▼                                    ▲
           ┌──────────────────────────┐                  │
           │ Employees enter sales    │                  │
           │ into ICS                 │                  │
           └──────────────────────────┘                  │
                    │                                    │
                    ▼                                    │
           ┌──────────────────────────┐                  │
           │ Employees complete       │──────────────────┘
           │ sales transaction        │
           └──────────────────────────┘
```

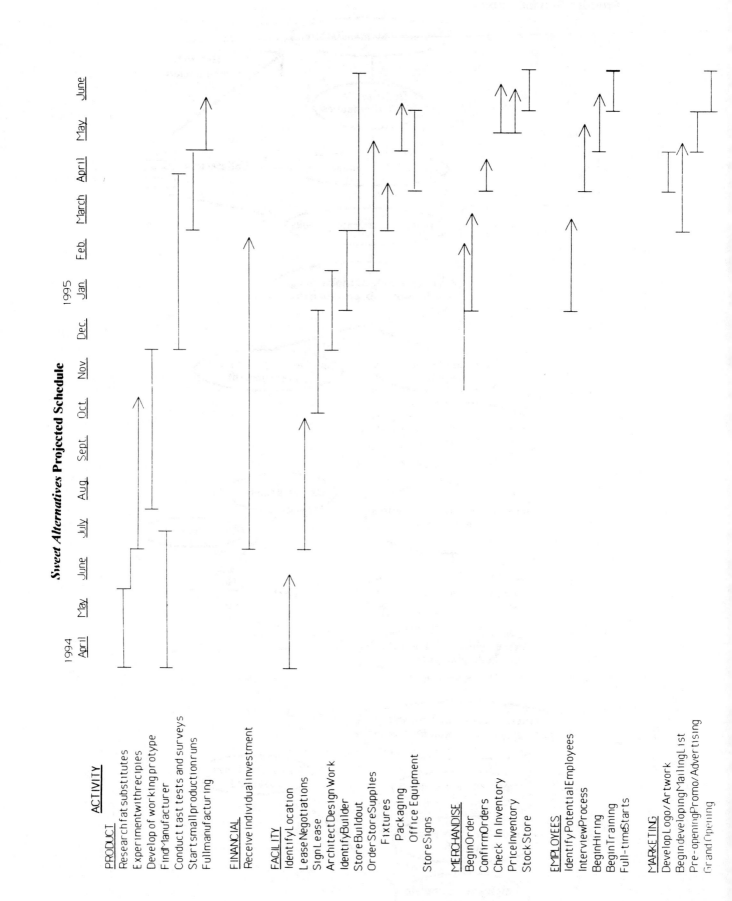

Risk Analysis and Alternative Plans of Action

<u>Sales Predictions Prove Wrong</u>

If sales predictions continued to prove wrong, *Sweet Alternatives* will reevaluate every aspect of the business. Costs will be cut wherever possible. The following are some possible budget cuts:

- Management bonuses will be reduced

- Marketing/Advertising expenses will be cut. *Sweet Alternatives* will prepare and print all marketing materials personally using computer software

- Health and Baking magazine subscriptions will be put on hold. We will send more press releases to these magazines.

- Management salaries will be reduced

- Sales force will be cut down

<u>Unfavorable Industry Trends</u>

There is a possibility that the low-fat craze may become less desirable to our consumers.

- FDA restrictions on fat substitutes could alarm the public

- Other substitutes could taste better than our product

- The market could stop being health conscious

We will combat these possibilities through our advertising:

- *Sweet Alternatives* will emphasize "all natural" products

- *Sweet Alternatives* will focus on the great taste of our product and how it will satisfy the consumer's craving for a delicious snack.

- *Sweet Alternatives* will bring in compliments such as ice cream, yogurt and muffins

- If the low-fat craze continues to decrease, *Sweet Alternatives* will introduce higher fat products to satisfy the consumer's need for higher fat snacks.

- *Sweet Alternatives* will continue R&D to keep up with the changing trends of the industry and the changing needs of the consumer.

Manufacturing Costs Increase

If manufacturing costs of our product become to expensive, *Sweet Alternatives* will look for other manufacturers to produce our cookies and brownies. In the event that every manufacturer and supply company raises the price, we will find a way to produce our product ourselves. The manner in which we produce our product will continue to meet all health department standards.

Competition Increases

Our attack on competition will be through our marketing and advertising. Currently, most of our competition does not invest in any advertising. This puts *Sweet Alternatives* at an advantage from the very beginning. If price wars do develop, the following options are possible attack plans:

- *Sweet Alternatives* will create competitive promotions to compete with other companies.

- *Sweet Alternatives* will introduce new products such as our ice cream cookie sandwiches, mini dough bites and cookie bars to entice customers to continue to choose our product over our competition.

- *Sweet Alternatives* will decrease prices if necessary

- If *Sweet Alternatives* is very threatened, new distribution systems will be developed. *Sweet Alternatives* can try to sell its recipe to other bakeries, cookie stores and grocery stores to keep their product available to the market.

Labor Decreases
If the labor force decreases, *Sweet Alternatives* will:
- increase employee's wage but cut down on the hours needed from each employee

- increase management hours until employees are available

- offer a small percentage of stock in the company to motivate workers to remain with the company and influence new employees to become a part of the *Sweet Alternatives* team.

Supply Decreases
As supply decreases, *Sweet Alternatives* will increase R&D to find other fat substitutes that continue to make our product enticing to our consumer. *Sweet Alternatives* will also look for other products to introduce that do not use the limited supply.

Capital is not available
Sweet Alternatives has faith in our advisory board and our investors. If a need for additional capital arises, we will consult them first. If this does not prove profitable, *Sweet Alternatives* will take the following steps:
- Upon starting *Sweet Alternatives*, costs will be cut until we have enough capital to begin production.

- Used equipment will be purchased

- *Sweet Alternatives* will approach different, potential investors with our concept

- *Sweet Alternatives* will look into bank loans

- In the event that *Sweet Alternatives* is not able to open their doors, we will look for new ways to distribute our product.

    1. Use carts to sell our product

    2. Sell concept to other manufacturer

Government Interferences

Currently the possible government interferences that can effect our operation are the health care reform bill, any new health department regulations and new taxes. If these impact our business, *Sweet Alternatives* will:

- Provide the least amount of coverage possible for our full time employees

- Provide no extra health benefits for part-time employees

- Conform to any new Health Department rules and regulations. This will allow the company to continue its services in a sanitary manner.

- Increase prices with increasing taxes.

Product Liability

The rapport of *Sweet Alternatives* is very important. In event that a product liability problem arises, *Sweet Alternatives* and its owners will do everything possible to investigate the problem and make our product reliable once again. The following are actions that will help rebuild consumer confidence in *Sweet Alternatives*:

- Increase Marketing and Advertising to establish a new rapport with the community

- Compensate any person effected by our product liability to ensure their needs are met

- Increase R&D to ensure our product is safe

- Increase lawyer fees to cover liability responsibilities.

Management/Personnel Problems

All management and personnel problems will be dealt with directly. Management will look into every problem separately and determine the cause of the conflict. If it is a problem that can be solved with a simple meeting to vent frustration, it will be held immediately. Larger problems will have more serious repercussions:

- Steeling from *Sweet Alternatives* will not be tolerated. The culprit will be terminated immediately.

- Inefficient work will be reviewed and discussed.

- If the employee does not change his/her actions they will be terminated with two weeks notice.

- Disrespect to customers will not be tolerated

- If the employees actions do not change after one warning he/she will be terminated with two weeks notice.

In regards to management problems, a business consultant will be asked to evaluate each situation. The consultants recommendations will be seriously considered and the proper actions will be taken.

In the event an owner would like to severe their involvement with *Sweet Alternatives*, they will be bought out by the remaining owners and made to abide by all contracts and agreements.

See Appendix Exhibit A-1 thorugh A-7

Product Development Increases

Product development should not be a problem for *Sweet Alternatives*. We currently have several working prototypes and expect the development of further products to go just as smoothly. In regards to introducing new products after *Sweet Alternatives* is open, no product will be introduced until it is completely finished. This may push some of our deadlines for introducing a new product, however *Sweet Alternatives* feels it is important to ensure that every product they sell is perfect.

Salvaging Assets

In the event that *Sweet Alternatives* is unable to open its doors in June of 1995, the following will be salvaged:

- All equipment and smallwares and other assets will be sold back to Charlie's fixtures: 50% of the original price.

- *Sweet Alternatives* will sell its concept along with all recipes and forecasts

- *Sweet Alternatives* will sell its recipe to a large manufacturer in the cookie industry such as Nabisco or Keebler

- All packaging and paper products will be recycled

Growth
Plan

GROWTH PLAN

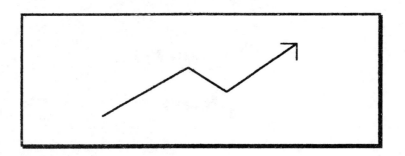

New Offerings to Market
  <u>Future Product/Services</u>

<u>6th Month</u>
- Introduce Discount Cookie Cards

<u>1st Year</u>
- Mini dough bites, Cookie ice cream sandwiches, Muffins

- T-shirts and Mugs with *Sweet Alternatives* trademark

<u>3rd Year</u>
- Move location directly on the Promenade

- Wholesale distribution

- Delivery to local businesses

- Fax orders

<u>New Marketplaces</u>

New Products/Service	Marketplace
Wholesale Distribution	• College Campuses • Health Clubs • Coffee Houses
Delivery	• Local businesses
Fax Orders	• Local businesses

Capital Requirements

Obtaining Future Capital

- Equity: We will look for new investors to help support improving the growth of *Sweet Alternatives*

- Each owner will invest an equal amount of equity to raise the needed capital

- Due to the moratorium on the Promenade, if Sweet Alternatives decides to move directly on to the Promenade, they will have to buy out an already existing space for the key money price, currently: $150,000. We will obtain this as stated above.

Personnel Requirements

Job Title	Job Description	Salary	Benefits
Sales Manager	• Oversees store operations • Opens/closes store • Monitors employees	$50,000/ year	• Life insurance coverage
Delivery person	• Delivers pre-orders to local businesses	Minimum Wage	• 25% Product discounts • Free cookies at end of the day • Contest Rewards • Education of product & industry • Customer Service Training

Exit Strategy

- Sell for cash to an outside buyer
- Transfer stocks to other investors
- Sell concept to larger manufacturer for cash and royalties
- Sell *Sweet Alternatives* for key money. This will happen only if *Sweet Alternatives* is directly on the Promenade and we can sell our space to another company. *Sweet Alternatives* will receive $150,000 for it's space.

Financial Plan

Cash Flow Assumptions

1. <u>Retail Sales & Collections</u>

   Forecast:
January	$20,300
February	$22,400
March	$20,300
April	$20,300
May	$22,400
June	$28,000
July	$28,000
August	$26,600
September	$26,600
October	$20,300
November	$30,800
December	$33,600

Sales for each month will increase by ten percent (10%) in both years two and three.

Basis: Market research by South Coast Plaza Marketing department indicates that, on average, retail stores make approximately 60% of sales in the last two months of the year, mainly because of the "Christmas Rush". In addition to this holiday, Valentine's Day, Father's Day, Mother's Day, and "Back to School" cause the months of February, June, May, August and September to show increases in sales.

Comparison of these statistics, with our research of ten retail cookie stores in high "foot traffic" areas, shows that *Sweet Alternatives* will sell approximately the numbers shown. The monthly sales figures include cookies, brownies and beverages.

Collections of all sales will be made COD at the *Sweet Alternatives* retail store.

See Appendix Exhibit B-1

2. Investment Capital

These funds represent the initial equity in *Sweet Alternatives*. And will be provided by the management team in equal portions.

3. Purchases

Forecast:
January	$4,466
February	$4,928
March	$4,466
April	$4,466
May	$4,928
June	$6,160
July	$6,160
August	$5,852
September	$5,852
October	$4,466
November	$6,776
December	$7,392

Basis: Research of ten cookie stores in high "foot traffic" areas show that *Sweet Alternatives* will spend 22% of sales on production costs. These costs include packaging costs.

Purchases will be paid to our manufacturer on a Net 30 basis, and the cost will increase by ten percent (10%) in both years two and three.

See Appendix Exhibit B-1

4. Accounting

As quoted by Janet Garner (Independent CPA), accounting costs will be $250 per month for bookkeeping fees and $500 in February for tax return fees. All payments will be made on a Net 30 basis.

See Appendix Exhibit B-1

5. Legal

Legal costs for *Sweet Alternatives* have been estimated to be $2,000 up front plus $100 per month. Monthly costs will be paid on a Net 30 basis.

See Appendix Exhibit B-1

6. *Sweet Alternatives* Lease

Locations immediately surrounding the Bayside District of Santa Monica cost approximately $3.00 per square foot. Sweet Alternatives will occupy a 600 square foot space in this area. For a five year lease, *Sweet Alternatives* will be paying $1,800 per month with five months free rent. A rent increase of approximately 5% will occur in years two and three.

See Appendix Exhibit B-1

7. *Sweet Alternatives* Lease Deposit

Sweet Alternatives will be required to deposit $5,400 before occupying the space. This deposit includes first and last months rent plus an amount equal to the first months rent.

See Appendix Exhibit B-1

8. Vending Cart Lease

Sweet Alternatives will also rent a vending cart to be located on 3rd Street. For a five year lease, we will pay $500 per month. A rent increase of approximately 5% will occur in years two and three.

See Appendix Exhibit B-1

9. Vending Cart Lease Deposit

Sweet Alternatives will pay first and last months rent plus an amount equal to the first months rent as a deposit for use of the vending cart.

See Appendix Exhibit B-1

10. General & Administrative Costs.

General and Administrative cost include office supplies, employee handbook printing, *Sweet Alternatives* employee training programs, and food service training programs. *Sweet Alternatives* will have a $250 start-up cost plus a monthly replacement cost of $100.

11. General Supplies

Supplies include all cleaning supplies, baking materials, first aid materials, aprons, plastic gloves, wax paper, etc. *Sweet Alternatives* will have a $200 start-up cost plus a monthly replacement fee of $100 per month.

12. Life Insurance

As quoted by Prudential Insurance, a $100,000 term life insurance policy for each owner will cost $40 per quarter (26% of the annual premium). This premium will be fixed for 7 years.

See Appendix Exhibit B-1

13. Product Liability Insurance

As quoted by Cigna Insurance, *Sweet Alternatives* will be covered under their Business Owner's Policy. This includes General Commercial Liability, Contents Coverage, and Business Loss of Income. Costs will include: 1) $4.02 per every $1,000 in sales, and 2) $1.25 per $100 of capital. These costs will be paid quarterly.

See Appendix Exhibit B-1

14. Cooking Equipment

As quoted by Charlie's Fixtures, smallwares will cost approximately $400 up-front plus a replacement cost of $100 each quarter.

See Appendix Exhibit B-1

15. Leased Equipment

Sweet Alternatives will lease one espresso machine at $258 per month from Bravo Coffee Distributors.

See Appendix Exhibit B-1

16. Full Time Salaries

Sweet Alternatives will pay each of the four members of its management team $1,666 per month. These salaries will assume a 3 percent cost of living adjustment each year.

17. Full Time Wages

Sweet Alternatives will employ two individuals on a full time basis (no more than 40 hours per week). These employees will receive $8 per each hour worked every month. One full time employee will be added in year three.

18. Part Time Wages

Sweet Alternatives will employ one individual on a part-time basis (no more than 12 hours per week). This employee will receive $8 per each hour worked every month. One part-time (no more than 12 hours per week) employee will be added in year three. This employee will be paid $4.25.

19. Workman's Compensation Insurance Annual Deposit.

As quoted by State Fund Insurance, *Sweet Alternatives* will pay a $1,515 deposit at the beginning of the policy. This cost is based upon 35 percent of the estimated annual labor costs for the first year. The cost for years two and three will based upon 35 percent of the past years annual labor costs, and will occur on an annual basis from the beginning date of the policy. Because the management team will keep *Sweet Alternatives* labor costs fixed for the first three years, this annual insurance cost will remain at $1,515 per year.

See Appendix Exhibit B-1

20. Workman's Compensation Insurance Quarterly Payment

As quoted by State Fund Insurance, *Sweet Alternatives* will pay $9.78 per $100 paid to employees (not including full-time salary) each quarter.

See Appendix Exhibit B-1

21. Labor Taxes

Sweet Alternatives will pay approximately 11.25 percent of labor costs for labor taxes.

22. Advertising & Marketing

Forecast:
January	$500
February	$800
March	$500
April	$500
May	$800
June	$800
July	$800
August	$1000
September	$1000
October	$500
November	$1,700
December	$1,700

Basis: Advertising Costs include standard brochures ($0.23 per copy), glossy brochures ($0.75 per copy), and standard flier ($0.03 per copy), and newspaper adds. Costs vary with respect to sales volume.

23. Telephone

Using information provided by Pacific Bell, *Sweet Alternatives* estimates telephone costs at $150 per month with a one time start-up fee of $30. This cost assumes one telephone line with call-waiting. These costs will remain relatively fixed throughout the year.

24. Utilities

As quoted by the Electric Company and the Gas Company, *Sweet Alternatives* estimates utilities as averaging $1,000 per month. *Sweet Alternatives* has confirmed this number with retail cookie stores in similar areas. These cost will be paid on a Net 30 basis, and will increase by 10 percent in years two and three.

25. Research and Development

Sweet Alternatives Research and Development plan will cost approximately $500 per quarter.

See Product/Service Plan for detailed information

26. Licenses & Trademarks

Sweet Alternatives will pay licensing fees upon start-up of $1,500. These fees include filing Articles of Incorporation and Bylaws, a Fictitious Business Name, and Trademark Processing Fees.

27. Large Equipment

As quoted by Charlie's Fixtures, initial equipment costs have been estimated at $20,000.

See Appendix Exhibit C-9

28. Build-Out

Average cost of fixture, furniture, and walk-in is $75,000. This figure includes fixtures, furniture, walk-in, architecture, and interior designing costs. *Sweet Alternatives* has verified this figure with various architects, contractors, and interior designers.

See Appendix Exhibit B-1

Year 1

Ref#	Item	Premise	Start-Up	June	July	August	September	October	November	December	January	February	March	April	May	Totals	Percentage
	Cash In:																
1	Collections																
	Retail Sales			$28,000	$28,000	$26,600	$26,600	$20,300	$30,800	$33,800	$20,300	$22,400	$20,300	$20,300	$22,400	$299,800	70.58%
2	Investment Capital																
	Stock		$125,000													$125,000	29.44%
	Total Cash In:		$125,000	$28,000	$28,000	$26,600	$26,600	$20,300	$30,800	$33,800	$20,300	$22,400	$20,300	$20,300	$22,400	$424,600	100.00%
	Cash Out:																
3	Purchases																
	Net 30				$6,160	$6,160	$5,862	$5,862	$4,468	$8,778	$7,392	$4,468	$4,928	$4,468	$4,468	$60,984	16.35%
4	Accounting																
	Tax Return Fee	$500														$500	0.13%
	Bookkeeping	$250			$250	$250	$250	$250	$250	$250	$250	$250	$500	$250	$250	$2,750	0.74%
5	Legal	$100	$2,000		$100	$100	$100	$100	$100	$100	$100	$100	$100	$100	$100	$3,100	0.83%
	Fixed Costs																
	Sweat Alt. Rent																
6	Lease	$1,800							$1,800	$1,800	$1,800	$1,800	$1,800	$1,800	$1,800	$12,600	3.38%
7	Lease Deposit	$6,400	$5,400													$5,400	1.45%
	Vending Cart	$500														$0	0.00%
8	Lease							$500	$500	$500	$500	$500	$500	$500	$500	$1,500	0.40%
9	Lease Deposit	$1,500	$1,500													$1,450	0.39%
10	General & Admin	$100	$250	$100	$100	$100	$100	$100	$100	$100	$100	$100	$100	$100	$100	$1,400	0.38%
11	General Supplies	$100	$200	$100	$100	$100	$100	$100	$100	$100	$100	$100	$100	$100	$100		
	Insurance																
12	Life Ins.	$160		$160			$160			$160			$160			$640	0.17%
13	Liability Ins.						$632			$512			$607			$1,551	0.42%
14	Cooking Eq.						$100			$100			$100			$700	0.19%
15	Leased Equipment	$268	$400	$268	$268	$268	$268	$268	$268	$268	$268	$268	$268	$268	$268	$3,098	0.83%
	Salaries & Wages																
16	Full Time Salary	$8,333		$8,333	$8,333	$8,333	$8,333	$8,333	$8,333	$8,333	$8,333	$8,333	$8,333	$8,333	$8,333	$99,996	26.80%
17	Full Time Wages	$2,560		$2,560	$2,560	$2,560	$2,560	$2,560	$2,560	$2,560	$2,560	$2,560	$2,560	$2,560	$2,560	$30,720	8.23%
18	Part Time Wages	$384		$384	$384	$384	$384	$384	$384	$384	$384	$384	$384	$384	$384	$4,608	1.24%
19	Workman's Comp																
	Premium	$1,515	$1,515													$1,515	0.41%
20	Quarterly Rate	11.25%					$864			$864			$864			$2,591	0.69%
	Labor Tax			$1,002	$1,002	$1,002	$1,002	$1,002	$1,002	$1,002	$1,002	$1,002	$1,002	$1,002	$1,002	$12,029	16.04%
	Variable Costs																
22	Adv. & Marketing			$800	$800	$1,000	$1,000	$500	$1,700	$1,700	$500	$800	$500	$500	$800	$10,600	2.84%
23	Telephone	$150	$30	$150	$150	$150	$150	$150	$150	$150	$150	$150	$150	$150	$150	$1,830	0.49%
24	Utilities	$1,000		$1,000	$1,000	$1,000	$1,000	$1,000	$1,000	$1,000	$1,000	$1,000	$1,000	$1,000	$1,000	$12,000	3.22%
25	R&D	$500					$500			$500			$500			$1,500	0.40%
26	Licenses		$1,500													$1,500	0.40%
27	Capital Equipment		$20,000													$20,000	5.36%
28	Build Out		$75,000													$75,000	20.10%
	Total Cash Out:		$107,795	$14,847	$21,197	$21,397	$23,245	$20,589	$22,703	$27,150	$24,429	$21,803	$24,596	$21,503	$21,803	$373,080	100.00%
	Cash Position (Monthly)		$17,205	$13,153	$6,803	$5,203	$3,366	($289)	$8,097	$6,450	($4,129)	$597	($4,296)	($1,203)	$597	$51,540	
	Cash Position (Fiscal Period)		$17,205	$30,358	$37,160	$42,363	$45,718	$45,428	$53,525	$59,975	$55,846	$56,442	$52,147	$50,943	$51,540		
	Cash Position (Forwarded to Yr. 2)															$51,540	

Year 2

Ref#	Item		Start-Up	Premise	June	July	August	September	October	November	December	January	February	March	April	May	Totals	Percentage
	Cash In:																	
1	Collections																	
	Retail Sales				$30,800	$30,800	$29,260	$29,260	$22,330	$33,880	$36,960	$22,330	$24,640	$22,330	$22,330	$24,640	$329,560	100.00%
2	Investment Capital																	
	Stock																$0	0.00%
	Total Cash In:				$30,800	$30,800	$29,260	$29,260	$22,330	$33,880	$36,960	$22,330	$24,640	$22,330	$22,330	$24,640	$329,560	100.00%
	Cash Out:																	
3	Purchases																	
	Net 30				$4,928	$6,776	$6,776	$6,437	$6,437	$4,913	$7,454	$8,131	$4,913	$5,421	$4,913	$4,913	$72,010	24.10%
4	Accounting																	
	Tax Return Fee	$500												$500			$500	0.17%
	Bookkeeping	$250			$250	$250	$250	$250	$250	$250	$250	$250	$250	$250	$250	$250	$3,000	1.00%
5	Legal	$100			$100	$100	$100	$100	$100	$100	$100	$100	$100	$100	$100	$100	$1,200	0.40%
	Fixed Costs																	
	Sweat Alt. Rent																	
6	Lease	$1,890			$1,985	$1,985	$1,985	$1,985	$1,985	$1,985	$1,985	$1,985	$1,985	$1,985	$1,985	$1,985	$23,814	7.97%
7	Lease Deposit																$0	0.00%
	Vending Cart																$0	0.00%
8	Lease	$525			$551	$551	$551	$551	$551	$551	$551	$551	$551	$551	$551	$551		
9	Lease Deposit																$0	0.00%
10	General & Admin	$100			$100	$100	$100	$100	$100	$100	$100	$100	$100	$100	$100	$100	$1,200	0.40%
11	General Supplies	$100			$100	$100	$100	$100	$100	$100	$100	$100	$100	$100	$100	$100	$1,200	0.40%
	Insurance																	
12	Life Ins.	$160			$160			$160			$160			$160			$640	0.21%
13	Liability Ins.				$503			$615			$594			$587			$2,299	0.77%
14	Cooking Eq.				$100			$100			$100			$100			$400	0.13%
15	Leased Equipment	$268			$268	$268	$268	$268	$268	$268	$268	$268	$268	$268	$268	$268	$3,096	1.04%
	Salaries & Wages																	
16	Full Time Salary	$8,583			$8,583	$8,583	$8,583	$8,583	$8,583	$8,583	$8,583	$8,583	$8,583	$8,583	$8,583	$8,583	$102,996	34.48%
17	Full Time Wages	$2,560			$2,560	$2,560	$2,560	$2,560	$2,560	$2,560	$2,560	$2,560	$2,560	$2,560	$2,560	$2,560	$30,720	10.28%
18	Part Time Wages	$384			$384	$384	$384	$384	$384	$384	$384	$384	$384	$384	$384	$384	$4,608	1.54%
	Workman's Comp																	
19	Premium				$1,209												$1,209	0.40%
20	Quarterly Rate				$864			$864			$864			$864			$3,456	1.16%
	Labor Tax	11.25%			$1,025	$1,025	$1,025	$1,025	$1,025	$1,025	$1,025	$1,025	$1,025	$1,025	$1,025	$1,025	$12,295	4.11%
	Variable Costs																	
22	Adv. & Marketing				$800	$800	$1,000	$1,000	$500	$1,700	$1,700	$500	$800	$500	$500	$800	$10,600	3.55%
23	Telephone	$150			$150	$150	$150	$150	$150	$150	$150	$150	$150	$150	$150	$150	$1,800	0.60%
24	Utilities	$1,100			$1,100	$1,100	$1,100	$1,100	$1,100	$1,100	$1,100	$1,100	$1,100	$1,100	$1,100	$1,100	$13,200	4.42%
25	R&D	$500			$500			$500			$500			$500			$2,000	0.67%
26	Licenses																	
27	Capital Equipment																	
28	Build Out																	
	Total Cash Out:		$61,540		$26,209	$24,721	$24,921	$26,822	$24,093	$23,758	$28,516	$25,777	$22,858	$25,777	$22,558	$22,858	$298,868	100.00%
	Cash Position (Monthly)				$4,591	$6,079	$4,339	$2,438	($1,763)	$10,122	$8,444	($3,447)	$1,782	($3,447)	($228)	$1,782	$30,702	
	Cash Position (Fiscal Period)		$51,540		$56,130	$62,209	$66,548	$68,986	$67,233	$77,356	$85,799	$82,353	$84,135	$80,687	$80,459	$82,241		
	Cash Position (Forwarded to Year 3)																$82,241	

Year 3

Ref#	Item	Premise	Start-Up	June	July	August	September	October	November	December	January	February	March	April	May	Totals	Percentage
	Cash In:																
1	Collections																100.00%
	Retail Sales			$33,880	$33,880	$32,186	$32,186	$24,563	$37,268	$40,866	$24,563	$27,104	$24,563	$24,563	$27,104	$362,518	100.00%
2	Investment Capital																0.00%
	Stock															$0	
	Total Cash In:			$33,880	$33,880	$32,186	$32,186	$24,563	$37,268	$40,866	$24,563	$27,104	$24,563	$24,563	$27,104	$362,518	100.00%
	Cash Out:																
3	Purchases																
	Net 30			$5,420	$7,454	$7,454	$7,081	$7,081	$5,404	$8,199	$8,944	$5,404	$5,963	$5,404	$5,404	$79,211	23.69%
4	Accounting																
	Tax Return Fee	$500												$500		$500	0.15%
	Bookkeeping	$250		$250	$250	$250	$250	$250	$250	$250	$250	$250	$250	$250	$250	$3,000	0.90%
5	Legal	$100		$100	$100	$100	$100	$100	$100	$100	$100	$100	$100	$100	$100	$1,200	0.36%
	Fixed Costs																
	Sweet Alt. Rent																
6	Lease	$1,980		$1,980	$1,980	$1,980	$1,980	$1,980	$1,980	$1,980	$1,980	$1,980	$1,980	$1,980	$1,980	$23,760	7.11%
7	Lease Deposit															$0	0.00%
	Vending Cart															$0	0.00%
8	Lease	$550		$605	$605	$605	$605	$605	$605	$605	$605	$605	$605	$605	$605		
9	Lease Deposit															$0	0.00%
10	General & Admin	$100		$100	$100	$100	$100	$100	$100	$100	$100	$100	$100	$100	$100	$1,200	0.36%
11	General Supplies	$100		$100	$100	$100	$100	$100	$100	$100	$100	$100	$100	$100	$100	$1,200	0.36%
	Insurance																
12	Life Ins.	$160		$160			$160			$160			$160			$640	0.19%
13	Liability Ins.			$529			$652			$628			$621			$2,429	0.73%
14	Cooking Eq.			$100			$100			$100			$100			$400	0.12%
15	Leased Equipment	$258		$258	$258	$258	$258	$258	$258	$258	$258	$258	$258	$258	$258	$3,096	0.93%
	Salaries & Wages																
16	Full Time Salary	$8,840		$8,840	$8,840	$8,840	$8,840	$8,840	$8,840	$8,840	$8,840	$8,840	$8,840	$8,840	$8,840	$106,086	31.72%
17	Full Time Wages	$4,000		$4,000	$4,000	$4,000	$4,000	$4,000	$4,000	$4,000	$4,000	$4,000	$4,000	$4,000	$4,000	$48,000	14.35%
18	Part Time Wages	$588		$588	$588	$588	$588	$588	$588	$588	$588	$588	$588	$588	$588	$7,056	2.11%
	Workman's Comp																
19	Premium			$1,209												$1,209	0.36%
20	Quarterly Rate			$884			$1,346			$1,346			$1,346			$4,902	1.47%
	Labor Tax	11.25%		$1,194	$1,194	$1,194	$1,194	$1,194	$1,194	$1,194	$1,194	$1,194	$1,194	$1,194	$1,194	$14,324	4.28%
	Variable Costs																
22	Adv. & Marketing			$800	$800	$1,000	$1,000	$500	$1,700	$1,700	$500	$800	$500	$500	$800	$10,600	3.17%
23	Telephone	$150		$150	$150	$150	$150	$150	$150	$150	$150	$150	$150	$150	$150	$1,800	0.54%
24	Utilities	$1,210		$1,210	$1,210	$1,210	$1,210	$1,210	$1,210	$1,210	$1,210	$1,210	$1,210	$1,210	$1,210	$14,520	4.34%
25	R&D	$500		$500			$500			$500			$500			$2,000	0.60%
26	Licenses															$0	0.00%
27	Capital Equipment															$0	0.00%
28	Build Out															$0	0.00%
	Total Cash Out:			$28,957	$27,829	$27,829	$30,214	$26,956	$26,479	$32,008	$28,819	$26,579	$29,065	$26,279	$25,679	$334,393	100.00%
	Cash Position (Monthly)			$4,923	$6,251	$4,367	$1,972	($2,393)	$10,789	$8,648	($4,256)	$1,525	($4,502)	($1,716)	$1,525	$28,123	
	Cash Position (Fiscal Period)		$82,241	$87,165	$93,416	$97,773	$99,745	$97,352	$108,141	$116,789	$112,533	$114,058	$109,555	$108,839	$110,364		
	Cash Position (Forwarded to Yr. 4)														$110,364		

	June	July	August	September	October	November	December	January	February	March	April	May
Revenue	$28,000	$28,000	$26,600	$26,600	$20,300	$30,800	$33,600	$20,300	$22,400	$20,300	$20,300	$22,400
Cost of Goods Sold	$6,160	$6,160	$5,852	$5,852	$4,466	$6,776	$7,392	$4,466	$4,928	$4,466	$4,466	$0
Gross Profit	$21,840	$21,840	$20,748	$20,748	$15,834	$24,024	$26,208	$15,834	$17,472	$15,834	$15,834	$22,400
Operating Expenses												
Accounting	$0	$250	$250	$250	$250	$250	$250	$250	$250	$750	$250	$250
Legal	$0	$100	$100	$100	$100	$100	$100	$100	$100	$100	$100	$100
Rent	$2,300	$0	$0	$0	$0	$0	$0	$2,300	$2,300	$2,300	$2,300	$2,300
General and Administrative	$100	$100	$100	$100	$100	$100	$100	$100	$100	$100	$100	$100
General Supplies	$100	$100	$100	$100	$100	$100	$100	$100	$100	$100	$100	$100
Insurance	$150	$0	$0	$1,556	$0	$0	$1,536	$0	$0	$1,530	$0	$0
Cooking Equipment	$0	$0	$0	$100	$0	$0	$100	$0	$0	$100	$0	$0
Leased Equipment	$258	$258	$258	$258	$258	$258	$258	$258	$258	$258	$258	$258
Salaries and Wages	$11,277	$11,277	$11,277	$11,277	$11,277	$11,277	$11,277	$11,277	$11,277	$11,277	$11,277	$11,277
Labor Tax	$1,002	$1,002	$1,002	$1,002	$1,002	$1,002	$1,002	$1,002	$1,002	$1,002	$1,002	$1,002
Advertising and Marketing	$800	$800	$1,000	$1,000	$500	$1,700	$1,700	$500	$800	$500	$500	$800
Telephone	$150	$150	$150	$150	$150	$150	$150	$150	$150	$150	$150	$150
Utilities	$1,000	$1,000	$1,000	$1,000	$1,000	$1,000	$1,000	$1,000	$1,000	$1,000	$1,000	$1,000
Research and Development	$0	$0	$0	$500	$0	$0	$500	$0	$0	$500	$0	$0
Licenses	$0	$0	$0	$0	$0	$0	$0	$0	$0	$0	$0	$0
Depreciation	$1,583	$1,583	$1,583	$1,583	$1,583	$1,583	$1,583	$1,583	$1,583	$1,583	$1,583	$1,583
Total Operating Expenses	$18,730	$16,362	$16,820	$18,976	$16,320	$17,520	$19,657	$18,620	$18,920	$21,251	$18,620	$18,920
Earnings Before Taxes	$3,110	$5,478	$3,928	$1,772	($486)	$6,504	$6,551	($2,786)	($1,448)	($5,417)	($2,786)	$3,480
Taxes (30%)	$933	$1,643	$1,178	$532	$0	$1,951	$1,965	$0	$0	$0	$0	$1,044
Net Income (Loss)	$2,177	$3,834	$2,749	$1,240	($486)	$4,553	$4,586	($2,786)	($1,448)	($5,417)	($2,786)	$2,436

	Year 2	Year 3
Revenue	$329,560	$362,516
Cost of Goods Sold	$72,010	$79,211
Gross Profit	$257,550	$283,305

Operating Expenses		
Accounting	$3,500	$3,500
Legal	$1,200	$1,200
Rent	$30,426	$31,020
General and Administrative	$1,200	$1,200
General Supplies	$1,200	$1,200
Insurance	$5,533	$9,180
Cooking Equipment	$400	$400
Leased Equipment	$3,096	$3,096
Salaries and Wages	$138,324	$161,142
Lobor Tax	$12,295	$14,324
Advertising and Marketing	$10,600	$10,600
Telephone	$1,800	1800
Utilities	$13,200	$14,520
Research and Development	$2,000	$2,000
Licenses	$0	$0
Depreciation	$19,000	$19,000
Total Operating Expenses	$243,774	$274,182

Earnings Before Taxes	$13,776	$9,123
Taxes	$4,133	$2,737

Net Income (Loss)	$9,643	$6,386

APPENDIX

TABLE OF CONTENTS

Exhibit	A	Contract & Agreements, Regulations, and Insurance Policies
	A-1	Employee Non-compete Agreement (Specific Radius)
	A-2	Employee Secrecy Agreement
	A-3	Employee Confidentiality Agreement
	A-4a	Non-disclosure / Non-compete Agreement (Initial Start-up phase)
	A-4b	Non-disclosure / Non-compete Agreement (Growth Phase)
	A-5	Trademark Registration
	A-6	Confidentiality Disclosure Agreement
	A-7	Non-disclosure Agreement
	A-8	Confidential Disclosure Agreement
	A-9	Form SS-4: Federal Employer ID #
	A-10	Form DE-1: State Employer #
	A-11	Form 1120S: Federal S-Corp. Income Tax Return
	A-12	Form 100S: State S-Corp. Income Tax Return
	A-13	Form 8109-B: Federal Payroll & Corporate Tax Deposit
	A-14	Form DE-3M: State Payroll Tax Deposit
	A-15	Form 941: Federal Quarterly Payroll Tax Return
	A-16	Form 940: Federal Annual Unemployment Tax Return
	A-17	Form DE-3DP: State Quarterly Payroll Tax Return
	A-18	Form W-4
	A-19	Form W-2: Wage Statement for Employees
	A-20	CA Uniform Retail Food Facilities Law
	A-21	Health & Safety Code / CA Administrative Code
	A-22	Food Market Retail Inspection Procedure Guidelines

	A-23	**Construction Requirements For Retail Bakers**
	A-24	**Insurance Policy**
Exhibit	B	**References and Resumes**
	B-1	**References**
	B-2	**Resumes**
Exhibit	C	**Additional Information, Statistics, and Articles**
	C-1	**Fat Substitutes**
	C-2	**Secret Recipes**
	C-3	**Spin-offs**
	C-4	**Consumers Who Pay More For Healthier Products Graph**
	C-5	**Product Survey**
	C-6	**Survey Results**
	C-7	**Fliers and Coupons**
	C-8	**Articles**
	C-9	**Cooking Equipment and Capital Equipment Pricing List**

CHAPTER 2
WILL BULLAS, INCORPORATED

Written by:
    Erin Rosenwald for
    Bill and Jennifer Hill of Will Bullas, Incorporated

Computer hardware:
    Apple Macintosh

Computer software:
    Microsoft Word, Microsoft Excel

Printing:
    Kinko's Copies

Book used to write business plan :
    <u>The Entrepreneur's Planning Handbook</u>

Overview

The Entrepreneurship Program, School of Business Administration at the University of Southern California, was discussed in the Sweet Alternatives business plan overview. Erin Rosenwald was a student enrolled in USC's Entrepreneur Program. The Will Bullas, Incorporated business plan was developed by Erin during her second semester and was used as her individual business plan. This business plan was written for Will Bullas, Incorporated to determine if it would be feasible for this company to open a retail store selling Will Bullas art designs on a variety of different products (prints, clothing, ceramics, greeting cards, etc.).

The Will Bullas, Incorporated business plan was chosen because of its attractive design, appealing layout, and use of graphics. It was also chosen because it is illustrative of the critical areas that a retail business plan must cover, such as open-to-buy sections, store layout, categories of inventory, etc.

Some information in this plan could be deemed proprietary. Since this business plan could not be executed without the artist's permission, no information was deleted from the plan. Because of the amount of information contained in the Appendix, only the Table of Contents for the Appendix is included.

Erin's use of graphs, charts and white space, made this plan easy to read while presenting most of the required information necessary for a business plan. Products are now being developed by various licensees and Will Bullas retail stores plan to open in California in the near future. This business plan proved that with a minimum of sales volume, Will Bullas stores could be profitable and worth launching.

BUSINESS PLAN CRITIQUE

Name: Will Bullus, Incorporated

I. Overall Appearance and Format

Good use of the artist's paintings is made so the reader can see the potential of selling these images in a retail store. The plan incorporates charts and bullets effectively, which makes the plan easy to read. Length is appropriate for this type of venture--approximately 46 pages. Because of the length of the Appendix, only the Table of Contents for the Appendix is included, not all the exhibits.

II. Cover Page

Strength:

Products are illustrated attractively on the cover, which attracts the reader's attention.

III. Table of Contents

Strength:

The table includes each section in the plan as well as all the suggested subheadings. Page numbers are also included.

IV. Executive Summary

Strength:

It is written in letter form and addressed to the parties that would review the plan. It discusses how the funding would be acquired and documents what the investors would receive in return. When the entrepreneur is raising funds, it is important to highlight what is needed in the investment to make the proposed company successful.

Weakness:

The entrepreneur does not discuss the competition of other retail stores in Carmel, CA. This area is an extremely competitive market for retail businesses and competition should be addressed

BUSINESS PLAN CRITIQUE

V. Management and Organization

Weakness:

<u>Key Management</u>

Job descriptions are not complete and should include the duties that the CEO is responsible for, such as buying functions, selling, quality control, promotion, etc. The CEO's qualifications and expertise should be highlighted.

<u>Management and Organization Chart</u>

This chart does not show a store manager, although this position actually exists.

VI. Product/Service

Strength:

In a business plan for a retail store, the entrepreneur must include the product mix for the store. This is extremely important and is well described in this section. Including the categories of merchandise with percentages of total sales is very effective.

Weakness:

This section did not contain a store layout, which should be included in this section for any retail business. In addition, the type of fixtures, display cases, and other amenities that make up the atmosphere of the store should be mentioned.

VII. Marketing Plan

Strength:

All areas of the plan are included as well as identifying the customers and what kind of selling methods will be utilized.

BUSINESS PLAN CRITIQUE

Weakness:

<u>Gross Margin on Products</u>

This is not included in this section. The entrepreneur states that she anticipates receiving a 50% gross margin because she plans to double the wholesale price. However, this situation usually does not occur in a retail store because of shrinkage, which is discount sales, shop lifting, spoilage, returns, etc. The mistake made by most entrepreneurs with retail stores is not allowing for shrinkage in their inventory when writing their business plans. Therefore, the 50% gross margin in the plan will be lower.

VIII. Financial Plan

Strength:

<u>Assumptions</u>

The assumptions are thorough and support figures in the Cash Flow Statements. Also, the numbered assumptions correspond with the numbered entries on the Cash Flow Statements.

IX. Operating System

Strength:

All procedures for operating a retail store of this type are included. All contingencies are mentioned and solutions to potential problems are presented. The salvaging of assets subsection assists the investor in realizing how she or he might recoup their investments in case of failure.

X. Growth Plan

Strength:

It is very complete and the only one of the model business plans that thoroughly addresses the growth potential of the business. Not elaborating on the growth potential of the venture is a typical weakness of most business plans.

Will Bullas
Incorporated

The Retail Division

Business Plan 1992

The Will Bullas Store
Business Plan

■ Erin Rosenwald
CEO
6892 Seaway Circle
Huntington Beach, CA 92648
(714) 886-0518

Restriction on Disclosure of Data

The ideas and data contained within this business plan are exclusive property of the Will Bullas Store, Inc. and are disclosed in confidence for informational purposes only. They are not to be copied or duplicated in any form without the permission of author, Erin Rosenwald.

Will Bullas Store

Table of Contents

Executive Summary. . . . .

Management and Organization . . . .
    Board of Directors. . . . .
    Advisory Council. . . . .

Product Plan . . . .

Marketing Plan . . . .
    Competitive Matrix . . . .
    Customer Profile . . . .
    Pricing Profile . . . .

Financial Plan . . . .
    Assumptions . . . .
    Cash Flows . . . .
    Income Statements . . . .
    Balance Sheets . . . .

Operating System . . . .
    Administrative Policies . . . .
    Planning Chart . . . .
    Risk Analysis . . . .

Growth Plan . . . .
    Expansion . . . .
    Exit Strategy . . . .

Appendix Table of Contents . . . .

Dolores and Sixth
Carmel-by-the-Sea
(408) 649-0688

Executive Summary

Will Bullas Store

Executive Summary

March 24, 1992

Erin Rosenwald
6892 Seaway Circle
Huntington Beach, CA 92648
(714) 886-0518

New Masters Gallery
P.O. Box 7009
Carmel-by-the-Sea
California 93921

Dear Will, Bill, and Jennifer,

I wanted to thank you for taking the time to read my business plan for the Will Bullas Store, Inc. I believe there is a great opportunity working with Will Bullas and selling his licensed designs. Through focus groups we have found that people, young and old, find both the artist's characters and sense of humor to be quite creative and charming. Many agree that his designs would be well presented on all kinds of products. In a retail space the Will Bullas Store would exclusively display the Bullas prints, t-shirts, greeting cards and ceramics in a gallery type setting.

Currently, Will Bullas and his business associates are setting up the corporation, Will Bullas, Inc. The Will Bullas Store, Inc. will be set up as the retail division of the Will Bullas, Inc., yet be considered a separate entity as an S-Corporation. The plan was written to evaluate all aspects of opening the first Will Bullas Store and in the growth plan section, to look at expansion of the retail division.

As CEO, I believe that my retail experience, education, and high energy level will serve as a good foundation for this venture. In addition, I have put together an Advisory Council consisting of Accountants, Lawyers, Consultants, and experts in areas of the retail industry. I feel that each particular member is invaluable to the success of the Will Bullas Store and Corporation.

Dolores and Sixth
Carmel-by-the-Sea
(408) 649-0688

Will Bullas Store

Executive Summary

Living in Carmel last summer, I found this town to be an ideal location for a store of this kind. We would most easily reach our target market and benefit from Will Bullas' established reputation by opening the store in Carmel. Carmel attracts couples, families, business people, and art collectors from around the world. As Will Bullas' present opportunities with Greenwich Print House materialize, his name and characters will be recognized all over through nationwide distribution. This would be a golden opportunity to implement the growth plan to open Will Bullas Stores in many tourist areas as well as the option to franchise.

The Will Bullas Store, Inc. is looking for investors for a total contribution of $90,000 to fund beginning inventory, design of the store, and other start-up expenses. In return, the investors receive 70% ownership of the Will Bullas Store, Inc. and can expect a five year pay out of initial investment and return of 61% and higher by the fifth year of business. Each investor will be offered a seat on the Corporation's Board of Directors.

The Will Bullas Store, Inc. is presently in the start-up phase. The licensing and manufacturing entities are also in the process of being arranged. We expect to have licensing agreements made and products available by August. The store will be ready to open in January of '93.

Please consider this opportunity as you read through the business plan. I invite you to call me with any questions you may have.

Sincerely,

Erin Rosenwald, CEO
Will Bullas Store, Inc.

Dolores and Sixth
Carmel-by-the-Sea
(408) 649-0688

Management & Organization

Will Bullas Store

Management and Organization

KEY MANAGEMENT

CEO	Job Description: Responsible for moving the company in a positive direction to achieve the corporation's goals. Must understand all aspects of business and be able to work in all areas of the corporation.
Erin Rosenwald	Qualifications: Education in Entrepreneurship Retail Sales Experience Good understanding of licensing agreements Financial and management skills

See Appendix A for resume

COMPENSATION

Position	Salary	Benefits
CEO	$26,000	Ownership Medical Benefits
Store Manager Part time position	$12,000	Sales goal bonus

Dolores and Sixth
Carmel-by-the-Sea
(408) 649-0688

Will Bullas Store

Management and Organization

OWNERSHIP

Erin Rosenwald	30% ownership
Investors	70% ownership

See Appendix B for Shareholders' Agreement

Royalties

Will Bullas	10% of gross sales as royalties up to $300,000; 5% of sales thereafter

BOARD OF DIRECTORS

Erin Rosenwald	President
Bill Rosenwald	Secretary
Investors	To be elected at first Board Meeting

Dolores and Sixth
Carmel-by-the-Sea
(408) 649-0688

Will Bullas Store

Management and Organization

ADVISORY COUNCIL

Mentors	Title	Salary
Mack Davis	USC Professor of Entrepreneur Program (213) 740-0641	$300 per visit
Richard A. Honn	Attorney at Law Honn & Secof (213) 629-3900	$3000 for filing as Corporation
Marvin Reiter	CPA (714) 381-4471	No fee for Business Advice
Rubin Davila	USC Accounting Prof. (213) 740-5005	No consultation fee
Ed Hunter	Marketing Specialty in Advertising (303) 394-4478	Advertising Expense
Dreu Lawlor	Interior Designer (818) 285-3058	Consultation fee if needed

* Most Mentors will assist primarily in the start-up phase. A few Menors as noted will be helpful as consultants during the first two years of business.

Dolores and Sixth
Carmel-by-the-Sea
(408) 649-0688

Will Bullas Store

Management and Organization

INSURANCE

Life Insurance on CEO

    Company: Farmer's Insurance Group

    Agent: Tommy Contreras
               (714) 881-9593

    Type: Term Life Insurance
            Death Benefit of $500,000

    Cost: $50 per month, ten year level plan

Term Life Insurance may be converted to Whole Life at any time. Planning ahead this may be a good option for the corporation in five to ten years in order to build equity for capitalization.

EMPLOYEE INCENTIVE PLAN

The Incentive Plan consists of sales goals in order to maintain projected revenues and to drive the corporation's profit. For the Store manager there will be a pre-set monthly sales goal. When the monthly goal is met the store manager will receive the designated bonus. In most cases the bonus given will be a percentage of the sales above the monthly goal. For example if the goal for June is $30,000, the goal was met and sales at the end of the month hit $35,000. The goal was exceeded by $5,000 and the percentage for the bonus is 10%. The bonus of $500 will be given to the sales manager in terms of her sales contribution. If she had made 40% of the sales for June, her sales bonus for the month would be $200.

Daily, weekly, and monthly sales will be tracked by the daily sales sheets and the monthly goal sheet. The goal sheet is effective because both the store manager and CEO can visually have the goal in sight.

The Incentive Plan is more throughly explained as a reference for the store manager in the Training Manual. The daily sales sheet and monthly goal sheet are located in Appendix C.

Dolores and Sixth
Carmel-by-the-Sea
(408) 649-0688

Will Bullas Store

Management and Organization

MANAGEMENT ORGANIZATION
START-UP THROUGH 5 YEARS

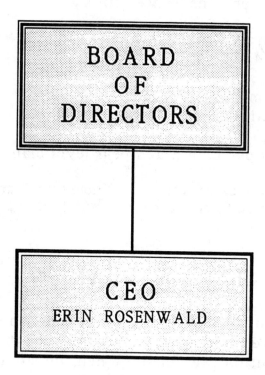

The Board of Directors will be aware of actions of the CEO through the Board's meetings, and therefore has control of the Corporation. Day to day operations are under control of the CEO, unless the Board finds it necessary to intervene. Futher responsibilities of Board of Directors and the relation to the Will Bullas Store is in included in the By Laws.

This corporation will be set up as a S Corporation in which the profits and losses will be passed to the owners of the corporation. The incorporation process will commence upon the first business transactions. The steps of the incorporation process, By Laws and Articles of Incorporation are included in Appendix D.

Dolores and Sixth
Carmel-by-the-Sea
(408) 649-0688

Product Plan

Frog Prints

Xmas Goose

Stuffed Animal

The Clip Art represents the art by Will Bullas

2-19

Will Bullas Store

Product Plan

Purpose of the Product

The Will Bullas Store will exclusively sell products with licensed designs by the artist, Will Bullas. The store display will create a gallery effect by showing various collectable items with the artist's characters and themes.

Product Mix

The product mix at this time consists of clothing, ceramics, greeting cards, stuffed animals, and prints. These items could be considered gift or collectable items. The combination of the original characters and the artist's humorous quotes make the artwork and products attractive and one of a kind.

T-shirts/Sweatshirts/Night Shirts	30%
Prints	25%
Cards	15%
Ceramics (Cups, Plates)	15%
Towels/Robes	10%
Xmas Ornaments	2.5%
Stuffed Animals	2.5%

Dolores and Sixth
Carmel-by-the-Sea
(408) 649-0688

Will Bullas Store

Product Plan

Unique Features

- Retail store with licensed products exclusively with Will Bullas' designs.

- The exclusive product mix creates a gallery effect.

- Will Bullas Store, Inc. has distribution rights to have a retail store and be the only retailer of Will Bullas licensed products within the city of Carmel. (Greeting cards and prints are exceptions) Contract to be negotiated.

- Contract with Will Bullas for special appearances at the Will Bullas Store for guest signings and public relations.

- Artwork by Will Bullas as store decor. The walls and counter of the store will be painted with Will's characters to enhance the presentation of products.

In addition to the unique features listed, one outstanding feature of this concept is that Will Bullas' art has been very successful in the current market. The annual Will Bullas shows in association with New Master's Gallery have attracted collectors from all over the world. Prior to the 5th annual show, approximately 90% of the show's painting had been sold. There has recently been much success with licensing of Will Bullas greeting cards with revenues in '91 approximately $250,000.

In 1992, the popularity and exposure of Will Bullas has the potential to be nationwide. Presently in negotiation with Greenwich Print House, Will Bullas may be presented as Greenwich's Artist of the Year. The exposure through prints and catalogs by Greenwich as well as the honor of being the artist of the year will benefit the artist as well as all licensing arrangements with his designs.

Dolores and Sixth
Carmel-by-the-Sea
(408) 649-0688

Will Bullas Store

Product Plan

Stage of Development

At this time, licensing negotiations are being set up between licensor and licensee for manufacturing of products. The licensing agreements and contracts for prints, towels/robes, and greeting cards have been established.

For the Will Bullas Store to begin operations, it is necessary to have all licensing contracts negotiated and to have products manufactured at a quality level prior to purchase of inventory. For this reason the retail division is now in a stage of planning and becoming an S-Corporation until products are available for purchase.

Trademarks, Copyrights, Royalties

Will Bullas™, the **Will Bullas Store**™, and **Will Bullas Designs**™ are trademarks of Will Bullas Store, Inc. and upon operations shall become registered trademarks, i.e. **Will Bullas**®.

The following have **copyright protection**:

- The Will Bullas Store Business Plan, © Erin Rosenwald, 1992
- Business forms including all sales documents and contracts

Royalties in 10% of net sales up to $300,000 and 5% thereafter will be paid to Will Bullas for use of his name, his designs, and for his appearences at the Will Bullas Store.

Distribution Rights for the Will Bullas Store to be the only retailer of Will Bullas licensed designs on products within the city of Carmel. Some exceptions apply. Contact to be negotiated.

Will Bullas Store

Product Plan

Product Limitation

The forseen limitations include quality and supply of products. The Will Bullas Store Inc. holds quality of products as an essential component of a successful business. The quality control of licensed products is the responsibility of the licensee. We would like to negotiate backup suppliers for the high volume products, such as t-shirts and sweatshirts, in order to insure supply quantities. A possible negative in terms of beginning inventory is that suppliers often require large orders especially when products are manufactured outside the United States.

Product Liability

General Business Policy insurance is necessary in order to cover liability of up to $1,000,000, fire and water damage, and business interuption.

    Company: Farmer's Insurance Group
    Agent: Scott Claus
    Type: General Business Policy
    Cost : $1200 per year

Related Services and Spinoffs

- Mail order catalog through the retail division.

- Changing market needs: The Will Bullas Store could easily adapt to a changing market by altering product mix and/or encouraging new products to be licensed and adding to product line. Ideas and illustrations of new products are in Appendix E.

- Will Bullas Store, Inc. will expand as a retail division by adding additional stores in various locations. However for the next five years the Corporation will focus on its Carmel-by-the-Sea location.

For further expansion plans, see Growth Plan.

Will Bullas Store

Product Plan

Environmental Factors

The Will Bullas Store, Inc. is environmentally conscious and responsible.

The beneficial environmental impact of Will Bullas Store, Inc. will include:

- Increase consciousness of animals and wildlife.

- Will Bullas' support of local causes and donation of designs.

- Environmental products could be created.

- All paper materials will be recycled including business forms, packaging, and gift bags.

Marketing Plan

Will Bullas Store

Marketing Plan/ Industry Profile

INDUSTRY PROFILE

Current Size

Products with licensed art have been successful for years. They most popularly include products such as greeting cards, prints, or photo books. Now art images can be reproduced on many mediums due to increased technology of image printing. Very well known artists such as Monet and Renoir have their images on cards, calendars, placemats, and similar items.

On a smaller scale, we can look at a specific artist to understand this type of industry. Laurel Burch of Laurel Burch, Incorporated has been very successful in the industry of reproducing images onto various products. The majority of her items are jewelry with other items as t-shirts and mugs. The Laurel Burch, Inc. is made up of two retail galleries, distribution and manufacturing entities and an international division. There has been much success thus far with Laurel Burch's 1991 sales of $18 million.

Growth Potential

Licensing is a very profitable and growing business today. With so many original works of art and so much creativity in the world, licensors make rather simple products have personality and style. An artist's individual look could lend itself to a scarf for example and be sold in the artist's gallery, specialty retail stores, or could be distributed to department stores.

Dolores and Sixth
Carmel-by-the-Sea
(408) 649-0688

Will Bullas Store

Marketing Plan/ Industry Profile

Geographical Location

Many cities nationwide have galleries and artwork exhibits within a sector of their tourist areas. For example, Carmel-by-tht-Sea, La Jolla, and Laguna Beach have local artist's works displayed in galleries and retail stores. Scared dog by Katie and Designs by Sally Huss are small stores in Melrose and Laguna respectively which exhibit works of art by the individual artist.

Seasonality

Seasonal impacts are extremely important in this industry, primarily as it relates to tourism. The typical locations for galleries, and thus artwork, are popular tourist towns so seasonality has a great impact on the number of visitors and most importantly sales. For most of these tourist towns, tourists and sales would be highest during vacation times (vacation time to be determined by city. Aspen would have different tourist peaks than San Diego) Art and other gift products or collectables have highest sales in months of peak tourism.

Profit Characteristics

The industry norm for retail items is 50% gross margin or keystone mark-ups. Mark-ups will vary from store to store.

Existing Distribution

Products with licensed artwork are sold in galleries and retail stores. There is increasing distribution to department stores where the products displayed are complementary and create a gallery effect.

Dolores and Sixth
Carmel-by-the-Sea
(408) 649-0688

Will Bullas Store

Marketing Plan/ Competition Profile

COMPETITION

Basis of Industry Competition

Creativity and attractive artwork is the basis of competition. The main competition for the Will Bullas Store is the Laurel Burch Galleries. Laurel Burch has found a market niche for her galleries in Carmel and Sausalito as well as through distribution to department stores. One advantage for Laurel Burch is the design of the galleries. The beautiful and exotic galleries often have tribal music playing to create quite a unique feeling. Laurel Burch has also gained popularity through her recognizable characters such as her cat designs.

COMPETITION MATRIX CHART

	Will Bullas Store	Laurel Burch, Inc.
Price	In terms of pricing strategy, Will Bullas' designs will be priced similar to competition's prices. Price should reflect quality.	Her prices are set to show value and originality of the artwork. Could be considered high prices but worth it.
Quality	QUALITY is priority	Laurel Burch items are high quality
Unique Features	Unique, attractive artwork; Appeal to all age groups	Colorful, abstract art designs
Distribution	The Will Bullas Store	Galleries; dist. to dept. stores; internat'l
Promotion	Local ads; Receptions: Press Releases; Future Mail Order	Catalog: Public Relations through community service
Location	Carmel-by-the-Sea	Carmel, Sausalito, Worldwide dist.
+Strengths -Weakness	+Many collectors of Will Bullas' paintings +Popularity in Carmel +Appeals to many -New to Industry	+Years of Experience in this industry +Established infastucture -Appeals to primarily to females -Sells more products, few paintings

Dolores and Sixth
Carmel-by-the-Sea
(408) 649-0688

Will Bullas Store

Marketing Plan

Competitive Advantage

- Unique art by Will Bullas
- Established name throughout Carmel
- Collectors worldwide
- The artwork appeals to people of all ages
- Excellent location
- Great management through infastructure
- Gallery with original paintings by Will Bullas nearby
- Nationwide distribution of prints through Greenwich Print House
- Success and exposure with licensed greeting cards

History of New Enterprises

According to Joe Dumbacher, head of licensing with Applause, Inc., there has been both success and failure in licensing and stores with licensed designs. The examples of successful licensing ventures include Walt Disney stores, Favia by Weedn Designs, Laurel Burch Galleries, and Ken Done Stores. However, there have been some disappointments in licensing arrangements, namely the Warner Brothers chain of retail stores. According to Joe Dumbacher, "For success in licensing, there needs to be appeal and admiration by large numbers."

Will Bullas Store

Marketing Plan/ Customer Profile

CUSTOMER PROFILE

Intented Customer

Previous Collectors	People who have purchased Will Bullas' art within the last five years. There are world wide collectors as well as local collectors.
New Customers	
Ages:	20-30 yrs. 50+ years
Sex:	75% female 25% male
Income:	$30,000 and above
Location:	Tourists as well as Carmel residents

Customer Benefits

- quality products
- unigue designs
- fashion
- art
- thoughful gifts
- mementos
- conversation pieces
- collectables
- humorous quotes

Market Niche

Sales projections and marketing analysis was based on our target market. The Carmel Chamber of Commerce provided the following information on Tourism:

Tourism		
	high	June 15th through mid. November
	mid season	February through mid. June
	down	mid. November through January

Dolores and Sixth
Carmel-by-the-Sea
(408) 649-0688

Will Bullas Store

Marketing Plan

Market Niche cont.

According to the tourism statistics by the Chamber of Commerce, we can predict sales to follow a similar pattern:

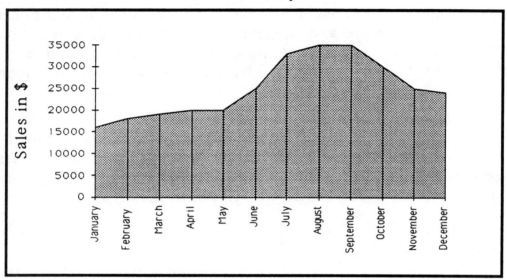

Sales for first year

Market Penetration

Will Bullas Retail Store
- A. Salespeople
- B. Receptions
- C. Guest Signings

Advertising
- A. Travel & Tourist Magazines
- B. Local Ads

Direct Mail
- A. Mailing List
- B. Brouchures
- C. Future Plans for Catalog

Dolores and Sixth
Carmel-by-the-Sea
(408) 649-0688

Will Bullas Store

Marketing Plan

Advertising and Promotion

- **Magazines**

Magazines that consist primarily of tourist infomation are very popular in Monterey Peninsula because of the high rates of tourism during the year. These magazines are helpful to tourists because they both advertise and suggest "hot spots" including restaurants, hotels, popular sights, shopping areas, and exhibits. Included in Appendix F is a cover donated by Will Bullas for a local magazine.

- **Local Advertisements**

Will Bullas art has been featured many times in *The Herald*, the newspaper for Monterey Peninsula. In addition to these press releases, some ads will be placed in the entertainment section of the paper. A recent article on Will Bullas is in Appendix G.

- **Mailing List**

The Will Bullas store will start generating a mailing list for all the customers and collectors of Will Bullas' artwork. From this mailing list we will be able to notify clients of new product lines and up coming events such as receptions and Will Bullas' guest signings. The mailing list will greatly benefit the retail division for plans of a catalog.

- **Brouchures**

Brouchures will be send to residents in the Carmel area as well as recent collectors of art. They will mainly be used to announce up coming events. Greeting cards by Will Bullas will also be used for promotion.

- **Receptions**

Receptions will be planned to promote the Will Bullas Store as well as the new designs and products. Will Bullas has agreed to do guest signing at these events. They are scheduled to be held in the months of June, September, and December.

Dolores and Sixth
Carmel-by-the-Sea
(408) 649-0688

Will Bullas Store

Marketing Plan

Budgets for Advertising

    Advertisements $650/month for first three years
    Receptions $1000 per show

FUTURE MARKETS

We will be able to reach new markets and expand the current market by doing the following:

- We can use the **initial products** to expand the market segment by convincing customers to use more or buy more often and by attracting new customers.

- Each year we plan to innovate with **new related products**. We will expand our product mix always keeping the quality and attractiveness of the original line.

- The retail division hopes to gain a **new market segment** by adding other retail locations in the years to come.

For futher expansion plans, see **Growth Plan**

PRICING PROFILE†

T-shirts	$26		Mugs	$14
Sweatshirts	$36		Collectors' Plates	$40+
Nightshirts	$30			
			Towels/Robes	$30
Prints				
unframed	$30-$200		Xmas Ornaments	$22
framed	$100-$450			
			Stuffed Animals	$26+
Greeting Cards	$1.35/each			

There will be at least a 50% gross margin on all products

†prices subject to change

Dolores and Sixth
Carmel-by-the-Sea
(408) 649-0688

Financial Plan

2-35

Will Bullas Store

Financial Plan

Assumptions

A. **Sales**

Sales based on tourism statistics by Carmel's Chamber of Commerce. Tourism is considered high in mid June until mid. November.; low mid. November through January; average during February through May. From this information we can predict the range of monthly sales over a five year period with conservative growth each year. See Appendix I for sales graph.

In addition, sales volume was based on actual location, traffic, and square footage of a retail store in Carmel. Through marketing and improvements in consumer awareness, sales per year are expected to increase from $300,000 the first year to $350,000 the second, to $380,000 the third. A new location of twice the size of the original store will allow for sales of $600,000 in the fourth year. Sales are expected to stablize in year five at $700,000.

B. **Collections**

All account receivables are COD to be paid by cash, check, or credit card.

C. **Inventory**

Inventory of $50,000 will be purchased in the start-up of the store. The level of inventory maintained will be based upon the sales for the next two to three months. Purchases will be made dependant on upcoming sales. See Appendix J for Inventory Turnover Ratios.

Dolores and Sixth
Carmel-by-the-Sea
(408) 649-0688

Will Bullas Store

Financial Plan

D. **Royalties**

Royalties will be paid to Will Bullas at the rate of 10% of net sales up to $300,000 and at the rate of 5% of net sales over $300,000.

E. **Costs associated with Start-up**

Start-up cost needed for the corporation are beginning inventory, rennovation and design of store, legal fees for incorporation, rent deposit, city licenses and permits, and dues & subscribtions. Additional inventory will be needed in year four due to the larger retail space and increase in sales.

Beginning Inventory		$50,000
Renovation/Design		
Year 1	$25,000	
(Year 4)	50,000	
		75,000
Rent Deposit		2,800
City Licenses/Permits		1,200
Dues/Subscriptions		400
Legal Fees		
Incorporation	$3,000	
Yearly Tax Prep.	700	
		3,700
Total Start-up		$83,100

F. **Capital Expenditures**

A Machintosh Power Book 140 2/40 will be purchased to maintain inventory and accounting records. Renovation in years 1 and 4 are considered capital expenditures as building improvements and store fixtures.

Dolores and Sixth
Carmel-by-the-Sea
(408) 649-0688

Will Bullas Store

Financial Plan

G. **Depreciation** — The computer has a useful life of ten years and will be depreciated using straight line depreciation. Lease Hold Improvements can be depreciated over the life of the lease. Store fixtures, shelfs, and furniture will be depreciated over their useful life of ten years.

Fixed Overhead

H. **Payroll** — Salary for the CEO, Store Manager and consultation charges for the Advisory Council members are included in the management section. In year four, there will be two part-time workers and in year five there will be three.

I. **Employee Taxes and Benefits** — The following taxes and benefits are based on both the full time and part time positions. Benefits are paid to cover FICA, Medicare, and Workers' Compensation.

State	4%
Federal	15%
Benefits	12%
Medical	$70/month

J. **Lease** — The retail space will be leased under a three year contract at $1400 per month. In year four the new location will have a lease contract with five year options for $4000 per month.

Dolores and Sixth
Carmel-by-the-Sea
(408) 649-0688

Will Bullas Store

Financial Plan

K. Operating Overhead — Operating supplies will be purchased as needed. Telephone is a fixed expense because few orders will be received by phone. Utilities, bank charges, dues and subscriptions are also included as operating expenses. These figures are based on an actual retail location in Carmel.

L. Insurance — General Business Policy to cover liabilities, fire and water damage, and business interuption will cost $1200 per year. Term Life Insurance for CEO is $50 each month, level for ten years.

M. Selling Expenses — All expenses related to sales are included in this catagory. Advertising, Shows & Receptions, Entertainment, and Car & Travel are selling expenses.

N. Contribution to Capital — An amount of net earnings from the cash flow documents will be used as contribution to capital during the first five years of operations. This is also referred to in the cash flows as Beginning Cash.

P. Income Tax — Because the corporation is set up as an S Corporation, income tax is paid on the earnings by the shareholders. Unlike federal rules, the California state rules there is still a tax imposed on the corporation (in addition to the tax on the individual shareholders) at a rate of 2.5% of corporate net income.

Dolores and Sixth
Carmel-by-the-Sea
(408) 649-0688

Will Bullas Store, Inc.
Cash Flow 1993

Description	Premise	Start-Up	January	February	March	April	May	June	July	August	September	October	November	December	Total	%
Action																
Sales in $	A		16,000	18,000	19,000	20,000	20,000	25,000	33,000	35,000	35,000	30,000	25,000	24,000	300,000	
Cash In																
Collections																
Retail	B		16,000	18,000	19,000	20,000	20,000	25,000	33,000	35,000	35,000	30,000	25,000	24,000	300,000	76.92%
Investment Capital	Stock @ $1 par	90,000													90000	23.08%
Total Cash In		$90,000	$16,000	$18,000	$19,000	$20,000	$20,000	$25,000	$33,000	$35,000	$35,000	$30,000	$25,000	$24,000	$390,000	100.00%
Cash Out																
Purchases Net 30	C															
			1,600	1,800	1,900	2,000	2,000	2,500	3,300	3,500	3,500	3,000	2,500	2,400	115,000	29.49%
Royalties	D														30,000	7.69%
Capital Expenditures	E,F															
Beginning Inventory		$50,000													50,000	12.82%
Renovation/Design		$25,000													25,000	6.41%
Computer		$2,500													2,500	0.64%
Payroll	H															
Full Time			2,200	2,200	2,200	2,200	2,200	2,200	2,200	2,200	2,200	2,200	2,200	2,200	26,400	6.77%
Part Time			1,000	1,000	1,000	1,000	1,000	1,000	1,000	1,000	1,000	1,000	1,000	1,000	12,000	3.08%
Advisory Council			300					300			300			300	1,200	0.31%
Taxes	I															
State			128	128	128	128	128	128	128	128	128	128	128	128	1,536	0.39%
Federal			480	480	480	480	480	480	480	480	480	480	480	480	5,760	1.48%
Benefits			454	454	454	454	454	454	454	454	454	454	454	454	5,448	1.40%
Lease	J		1,400	1,400	1,400	1,400	1,400	1,400	1,400	1,400	1,400	1,400	1,400	1,400	16,800	4.31%
Lease Deposit	E	$2,800													2,800	0.72%
Legal & Accounting	E	$3,000													700	3,700	0.95%
Utilities	K		140	140	140	140	140	140	140	140	140	140	140	140	1,680	0.43%
Phone	K		200	200	300	300	300	300	300	300	300	300	200	200	3,200	0.82%
Operating Supplies	K		2,000					1,000							3,000	0.77%
City Licensees/Permits	K	$1,200													1,200	0.31%
Bank Charges/Collections	K		288	324	342	360	360	450	594	630	630	540	450	432	5,400	1.38%
Dues/Subscriptions	K	$400													400	0.10%
Insurance	L		1,250	50	50	50	50	50	50	50	50	50	50	50	1,800	0.46%
Advertising	M		1,500			1,500			1,500			1,500			6,000	1.54%
Car/Travel	M		60	60	60	60	60	60	60	60	60	60	60	60	720	0.18%
Shows/Receptions	M							1,000			1,000			1,000	3,000	0.77%
Entertainment	M		250	200	100	100	100	100	100	100	100	100	100	150	1,500	0.38%
Total Cash Out		$84,900	$13,250	$8,436	$8,554	$10,172	$33,672	$11,562	$61,706	$10,442	$11,742	$51,352	$9,162	$11,094	$326,044	83.60%
Cash Position Monthly		$5,100	$2,750	$9,564	$10,446	$9,828	($13,672)	$13,438	($28,706)	$24,558	$23,258	($21,352)	$15,838	$12,906	$63,956	16.40%
Cash Position Fiscal		$5,100	$7,850	$17,414	$27,860	$37,688	$24,016	$37,454	$8,748	$33,306	$56,564	$35,212	$51,050	$63,956		

Will Bullas Store, Inc.
Cash Flow 1994

Description	Premise	January	February	March	April	May	June	July	August	September	October	November	December	Total	%
Action															
Sales In $	A	20,000	22,000	23,000	25,000	26,000	30,000	37,000	38,000	38,000	35,000	29,000	27,000	350,000	
Cash In															
Collections Retail	B	20,000	22,000	23,000	25,000	26,000	30,000	37,000	38,000	38,000	35,000	29,000	27,000	350,000	94.59%
Beginning Cash	N	20,000												20000	5.41%
Total Cash In		$40,000	$22,000	$23,000	$25,000	$26,000	$30,000	$37,000	$38,000	$38,000	$35,000	$29,000	$27,000	$370,000	100.00%
Cash Out															
Purchases Net 30	C		30,000			35,000		60,000			50,000			175,000	47.30%
Royalties	D	2,000	2,200	2,300	2,500	2,600	3,000	3,700	3,800	3,800	3,500	1,750	1,350	32,500	8.78%
Payroll	H														
Full Time		2,420	2,420	2,420	2,420	2,420	2,420	2,420	2,420	2,420	2,420	2,420	2,420	29,040	7.85%
Part Time		1,000	1,000	1,000	1,000	1,000	1,000	1,000	1,000	1,000	1,000	1,000	1,000	12,000	3.24%
Advisory Council			300			300			300				300	1,200	0.32%
Taxes	I														
State		137	137	137	137	137	137	137	137	137	137	137	137	1,642	0.44%
Federal		513	513	513	513	513	513	513	513	513	513	513	513	6,156	1.66%
Benefits		480	480	480	480	480	480	480	480	480	480	480	480	5,765	1.56%
Lease	J	1,400	1,400	1,400	1,400	1,400	1,400	1,400	1,400	1,400	1,400	1,400	1,400	16,800	4.54%
Legal and Accounting	E												700	700	0.19%
Utilities	K	140	140	140	140	140	140	140	140	140	140	140	140	1,680	0.45%
Phone	K	200	200	300	300	300	300	300	300	300	300	200	200	3,200	0.86%
Operating Supplies	K	2,000					1,000							3,000	0.81%
Bank Charges/Collections	K	360	396	414	450	468	540	666	684	684	630	522	486	6,300	1.70%
Dues/Subscriptions	K	400												400	0.11%
Insurance	L	1,250	50	50	50	50	50	50	50	50	50	50	50	1,800	0.49%
Advertising	M		1,500			1,500			1,500			1,500		6,000	1.62%
Car/Travel	M	60	60	60	60	60	60	60	60	60	60	60	60	720	0.19%
Shows/Receptions	M						1,000			1,000			1,000	3,000	0.81%
Entertainment	M	150	100	100	100	100	100	100	100	100	100	250	200	1,500	0.41%
Total Cash Out		$12,510	$40,896	$9,314	$9,550	$46,468	$12,140	$70,966	$12,884	$12,084	$60,730	$10,422	$10,436	$308,402	83.35%
Cash Position Monthly		$27,490	($18,896)	$13,686	$15,450	($20,468)	$17,860	($33,966)	$25,116	$25,916	($25,730)	$18,578	$16,564	$61,598	16.65%
Cash Position Fiscal		$27,490	$8,594	$22,279	$37,729	$17,261	$35,121	$1,155	$26,270	$52,186	$26,456	$45,034	$61,598		

2-41

Will Bullas Store, Inc.
Cash Flow 1995

2-42

Description	Premise	January	February	March	April	May	June	July	August	September	October	November	December	Total	%
Action															
Sales In $	A	24,000	25,000	25,000	28,000	28,000	35,000	40,000	40,000	38,000	37,000	31,000	29,000	380,000	
Cash In															
Collections															
Retail	B	24,000	25,000	25,000	28,000	28,000	35,000	40,000	40,000	38,000	37,000	31,000	29,000	380,000	96.20%
Beginning Cash	N	15,000												15000	3.80%
Total Cash In		$39,000	$25,000	$25,000	$28,000	$28,000	$35,000	$40,000	$40,000	$38,000	$37,000	$31,000	$29,000	$395,000	100.00%
Cash Out															
Purchases Net 30	C		35,000			35,000		65,000			55,000			190,000	48.10%
Royalties	D	2,400	2,500	2,500	2,800	2,800	3,500	4,000	4,000	3,800	2,700	1,550	1,450	34,000	8.61%
Payroll	H														
Full Time		2,662	2,662	2,662	2,662	2,662	2,662	2,662	2,662	2,662	2,662	2,662	2,662	31,944	8.09%
Part Time		1,000	1,000	1,000	1,000	1,000	1,000	1,000	1,000	1,000	1,000	1,000	1,000	12,000	3.04%
Taxes	I														
State		146	146	146	146	146	146	146	146	146	146	146	146	1,758	0.45%
Federal		549	549	549	549	549	549	549	549	549	549	549	549	6,592	1.67%
Benefits		509	509	509	509	509	509	509	509	509	509	509	509	6,113	1.55%
Lease	J	1,400	1,400	1,400	1,400	1,400	1,400	1,400	1,400	1,400	1,400	1,400	1,400	16,800	4.25%
Legal and Accounting	E												700	700	0.18%
Utilities	K	140	140	140	140	140	140	140	140	140	140	140	140	1,680	0.43%
Phone	K	200	200	300	300	300	300	300	300	300	300	200	200	3,200	0.81%
Operating Supplies		2,000					1,000							3,000	0.76%
Bank Charges/Collections	K	432	450	450	504	504	630	720	720	684	666	558	522	6,840	1.73%
Dues/Subscriptions	K	400												400	0.10%
Insurance	L	1,250	50	50	50	50	50	50	50	50	50	50	50	1,800	0.46%
Advertising	M		1,500			1,500			1,500			1,500		6,000	1.52%
Car/Travel	M	60	60	60	60	60	60	60	60	60	60	60	60	720	0.18%
Shows/Receptions	M						1,000			1,000			1,000	3,000	0.76%
Entertainment	M	150	100	100	100	100	100	100	100	100	100	250	200	1,500	0.38%
Total Cash Out		$13,299	$46,267	$9,867	$10,221	$46,721	$13,047	$76,637	$13,137	$12,401	$65,283	$10,575	$10,589	$328,047	83.05%
Cash Position	Monthly	$25,701	($21,267)	$15,133	$17,779	($18,721)	$21,953	($36,637)	$26,863	$25,599	($28,283)	$20,425	$18,411	$66,953	16.95%
Cash Position	Fiscal	$25,701	$4,434	$19,566	$37,345	$18,624	$40,577	$3,939	$30,802	$56,401	$28,118	$48,543	$66,953		

Will Bullas Store, Inc.
Profit and Loss Statement 1993

Description	Premise	January	February	March	April	May	June	July	August	September	October	November	December	Total	%
Gross Sales	A	16,000	18,000	19,000	20,000	20,000	25,000	33,000	35,000	35,000	30,000	25,000	24,000	300,000	100.00%
Less returns and allowances		320	360	380	400	400	500	660	700	700	600	500	480	6,000	2.00%
Net Sales		15,680	17,640	18,620	19,600	19,600	24,500	32,340	34,300	34,300	29,400	24,500	23,520	294,000	98.00%
Less Cost of Goods Sold															
Beginning Inventory		50,000	42,000	33,000	23,500	38,500	28,500	66,000	49,500	32,000	54,500	39,500	27,000	50,000	
Purchases		0	0	0	25,000	0	50,000	0	0	40,000	0	0	0	115,000	
Goods available for sale		50,000	42,000	33,000	48,500	38,500	78,500	66,000	49,500	72,000	54,500	39,500	27,000	599,000	
Ending Inventory		42,000	33,000	23,500	38,500	28,500	66,000	49,500	32,000	54,500	39,500	27,000	15,000	15,000	
Cost of goods sold		8,000	9,000	9,500	10,000	10,000	12,500	16,500	17,500	17,500	15,000	12,500	12,000	150,000	50.00%
Gross Margin		7,680	8,640	9,120	9,600	9,600	12,000	15,840	16,800	16,800	14,400	12,000	11,520	144,000	48.00%
Less expenses															
Royalties	D	1,568	1,764	1,862	1,960	1,960	2,450	3,234	3,430	3,430	2,940	2,450	2,352	29,400	9.80%
Payroll	H	3,500	3,200	3,200	3,200	3,200	3,500	3,200	3,200	3,500	3,200	3,200	3,500	39,600	13.20%
Payroll Taxes & Benefits	I	1,062	1,062	1,062	1,062	1,062	1,062	1,062	1,062	1,062	1,062	1,062	1,062	12,744	4.25%
Legal & Accounting	E	3,000											700	3,700	1.23%
Operating Expenses	K														
Lease		1,400	1,400	1,400	1,400	1,400	1,400	1,400	1,400	1,400	1,400	1,400	1,400	16,800	5.60%
Utilities		140	140	140	140	140	140	140	140	140	140	140	140	1,680	0.56%
Phone		200	200	300	300	300	300	300	300	300	300		200	3,200	1.07%
Operating Supplies		200												3,000	1.00%
City Licenses/Permits		1,200												1,200	0.40%
Insurance	L	288	324	342	360	360	450	594	630	630	540	450	432	5,400	1.80%
Bank Charges/Collections		1,250	50	50	50	50	50	50	50	50	50	50	50	1,800	0.60%
Selling Expenses	M														
Advertising		1,500			1,500		1,000	1,500		1,000	1,500		1,000	6,000	2.00%
Shows/Receptions														3,000	1.00%
Car/Travel		60	60	60	60	60	60	60	60	60	60	60	60	720	0.24%
Entertainment		250	200	100	100	100	100	100	100	100	100	100	150	1,500	0.50%
Depreciation	G	521	521	521	521	521	521	521	521	521	521	521	521	6,250	2.08%
Total expenses		17,939	8,921	9,037	10,653	9,153	12,033	12,161	10,893	12,193	11,813	9,633	11,567	135,994	45.33%
Net profit before taxes		(10,259)	(281)	83	(1,053)	447	(33)	3,679	5,907	4,607	2,587	2,367	(47)	8,006	2.67%
State income taxes[1]	P	0	0	2	0	11	0	92	148	115	65	59	0	200	0.07%
Net Earnings		($10,259)	($281)	$81	($1,053)	$436	($33)	$3,587	$5,759	$4,492	$2,522	$2,308	($47)	$7,806	2.60%

[1] The California rules for S Corporations generally follow the federal rules. However, California rule state there is still a tax imposed on the corporation at a rate of 2.5% of corporate net income.

Will Bullas Store, Inc.
Profit and Loss Statement 1994

Description	Premise	January	February	March	April	May	June	July	August	September	October	November	December	Total	%
Gross Sales	A	20,000	22,000	23,000	25,000	26,000	30,000	37,000	38,000	38,000	35,000	29,000	27,000	350,000	100.00%
Less returns and allowances		400	440	460	500	520	600	740	760	760	700	580	540	7,000	2.00%
Net Sales		19,600	21,560	22,540	24,500	25,480	29,400	36,260	37,240	37,240	34,300	28,420	26,460	343,000	98.00%
Less Cost of Goods Sold															
Beginning Inventory		15,000	35,000	24,000	12,500	35,000	22,000	67,000	48,500	29,500	60,500	43,000	28,500	15,000	
Purchases		30,000	0	0	35,000	0	60,000	0	0	50,000	0	0	0	175,000	
Goods available for sale		45,000	35,000	24,000	47,500	35,000	82,000	67,000	48,500	79,500	60,500	43,000	28,500	595,500	
Ending Inventory		35,000	24,000	12,500	35,000	22,000	67,000	48,500	29,500	60,500	43,000	28,500	15,000	15,000	
Cost of goods sold		10,000	11,000	11,500	12,500	13,000	15,000	18,500	19,000	19,000	17,500	14,500	13,500	175,000	50.00%
Gross Margin		9,600	10,560	11,040	12,000	12,480	14,400	17,760	18,240	18,240	16,800	13,920	12,960	168,000	48.00%
Less expenses															
Royalties	D	1,960	2,156	2,254	2,450	2,548	2,940	3,626	3,724	3,724	3,430	1,819	1,323	31,954	9.13%
Payroll	H	3,420	3,720	3,420	3,420	3,720	3,420	3,420	3,720	3,420	3,420	3,420	3,720	42,240	12.07%
Payroll Taxes & Benefits	I	1,130	1,130	1,130	1,130	1,130	1,130	1,130	1,130	1,130	1,130	1,130	1,130	13,560	3.87%
Legal and Accounting	E												700	700	0.20%
Operating Expenses	K														
Lease		1,400	1,400	1,400	1,400	1,400	1,400	1,400	1,400	1,400	1,400	1,400	1,400	16,800	4.80%
Utilities		140	140	140	140	140	140	140	140	140	140	140	140	1,680	0.48%
Phone		200	200	300	300	300	300	300	300	300	300	200	200	3,200	0.91%
Operating Supplies		2,000					1,000							3,000	0.86%
Bank Charges/Collections		360	396	414	450	468	540	666	684	684	630	522	486	6,300	1.80%
Insurance	L	1,250	50	50	50	50	50	50	50	50	50	50	50	1,800	0.51%
Selling Expenses	M														
Advertising			1,500			1,500			1,500			1,500		6,000	1.71%
Shows/Receptions							1,000			1,000			1,000	3,000	0.86%
Car/Travel		60	60	60	60	60	60	60	60	60	60	60	60	720	0.21%
Entertainment		150	100	100	100	100	100	100	100	100	100	250	200	1,500	0.43%
Depreciation	G	521	521	521	521	521	521	521	521	521	521	521	521	6,250	1.79%
Total expenses		12,591	11,373	9,789	10,021	11,937	12,601	11,413	13,329	12,529	11,181	11,012	10,930	138,704	39.63%
Net profit before taxes		(2,991)	(813)	1,251	1,979	543	1,799	6,347	4,911	5,711	5,619	2,908	2,030	29,296	8.37%
State income taxes[1]	P	0	0	31	49	14	45	159	123	143	140	73	51	732	0.21%
Net Earnings		($2,991)	($813)	$1,220	$1,930	$530	$1,754	$6,188	$4,788	$5,568	$5,479	$2,835	$1,979	$28,564	8.16%

[1] The California rules for S Coporations generally follow the federal rules. However, California rule state there is still a tax imposed on the corporation at a rate of 2.5% of corporate net income.

Will Bullas Store, Inc.
Profit and Loss Statement 1995

Description	Premise	January	February	March	April	May	June	July	August	September	October	November	December	Total	%
Gross Sales	A	24,000	25,000	25,000	28,000	28,000	35,000	40,000	40,000	38,000	37,000	31,000	29,000	380,000	100.00%
Less returns and allowances		480	500	500	560	560	700	800	800	760	740	620	580	7,600	2.00%
Net Sales		23,520	24,500	24,500	27,440	27,440	34,300	39,200	39,200	37,240	36,260	30,380	28,420	372,400	98.00%
Less Cost of Goods Sold															
Beginning Inventory		15,000	38,000	25,500	13,000	34,000	20,000	67,500	47,500	27,500	63,500	45,000	29,500	15,000	
Purchases		35,000	0	0	35,000	0	65,000	0	0	55,000	0	0	0	190,000	
Goods available for sale		50,000	38,000	25,500	48,000	34,000	85,000	67,500	47,500	82,500	63,500	45,000	29,500	616,000	
Ending Inventory		38,000	25,500	13,000	34,000	20,000	67,500	47,500	27,500	63,500	45,000	29,500	15,000	15,000	
Cost of goods sold		12,000	12,500	12,500	14,000	14,000	17,500	20,000	20,000	19,000	18,500	15,500	14,500	190,000	50.00%
Gross Margin		11,520	12,000	12,000	13,440	13,440	16,800	19,200	19,200	18,240	17,760	14,880	13,920	182,400	48.00%
Less expenses															
Royalties	D	2,352	2,450	2,450	2,744	2,744	3,430	3,920	3,920	3,724	2,946	1,519	1,421	33,620	8.85%
Payroll	H	3,662	3,662	3,662	3,662	3,662	3,662	3,662	3,662	3,662	3,662	3,662	3,662	43,944	11.56%
Payroll Taxes & Benefits	I	1,204	1,204	1,204	1,204	1,204	1,204	1,204	1,204	1,204	1,204	1,204	1,204	14,448	3.80%
Legal and Accounting	E												700	700	0.18%
Operating Expenses	K														
Lease		1,400	1,400	1,400	1,400	1,400	1,400	1,400	1,400	1,400	1,400	1,400	1,400	16,800	4.42%
Utilities		140	140	140	140	140	140	140	140	140	140	140	140	1,680	0.44%
Phone		200	200	300	300	300	300	300	300	300	300	200	200	3,200	0.84%
Operating Supplies		2,000					1,000							3,000	0.79%
Bank Charges/Collections		432	450	450	504	504	630	720	720	684	666	558	522	6,840	1.80%
Insurance	L	1,250	50	50	50	50	50	50	50	50	50	50	50	1,800	0.47%
Selling Expenses	M														
Advertising			1,500			1,500			1,500			1,500		6,000	1.58%
Shows/Receptions							1,000			1,000			1,000	3,000	0.79%
Car/Travel		60	60	60	60	60	60	60	60	60	60	60	60	720	0.19%
Entertainment		150	100	100	100	100	100	100	100	100	100	250	200	1,500	0.39%
Depreciation	G	521	521	521	521	521	521	521	521	521	521	521	521	6,250	1.64%
Total expenses		13,371	11,737	10,337	10,685	12,185	13,497	12,077	13,577	12,845	11,049	11,064	11,080	143,502	37.76%
Net profit before taxes	P	(1,851)	263	1,663	2,755	1,255	3,303	7,123	5,623	5,395	6,711	3,816	2,840	38,898	10.24%
State income taxes[1]		0	7	42	69	31	83	178	141	135	168	95	71	972	0.26%
Net Earnings		($1,851)	$257	$1,622	$2,686	$1,224	$3,221	$6,945	$5,483	$5,260	$6,543	$3,721	$2,769	$37,926	9.98%

[1] The California rules for S Corporations generally follow the federal rules. However, California rule state there is still a tax imposed on the corporation at a rate of 2.5% of corporate net income.

Will Bullas Store, Inc.
Balance Sheets

	1993	1994	1995	1996	1997
ASSETS					
Current Assets:					
Cash	61,500	59,500	68,000	72,000	145,000
Merchandise Inventory	15,000	25,000	15,000	25,000	20,000
Prepaid expenses	20,000	20,000	70,000	20,000	20,000
Fixed Assets:					
Computer	2,500	2,500	2,500	2,500	2,500
Less accumulated depreciation	-250	-500	-750	-1,000	-1,250
	2,250	2,000	1,750	1,500	1,250
Lease Hold Improvements	15,000	15,000	15,000	40,000	40,000
Less accumulated depreciation	-5,000	-10,000	-15,000	-4,000	-8,000
	10,000	5,000	0	36,000	32,000
Store Fixtures	10,000	10,000	10,000	20,000	20,000
Less accumulated depreciation	-1,000	-2,000	-3,000	-5,000	-7,000
	9,000	8,000	7,000	15,000	13,000
	$117,750	**$119,500**	**$161,750**	**$169,500**	**$231,250**
LIABILITIES & NET WORTH					
Current Liabilities					
Accounts Payable	0	0	0	45,000	85,000
Taxes Payable	7,750	9,500	3,750	14,500	26,250
Net Worth					
90,000 shares common stock	90,000	90,000	90,000	90,000	90,000
Contribution to Capital	20,000	20,000	68,000	20,000	30,000
	$117,750	**$119,500**	**$161,750**	**$169,500**	**$231,250**

Operating System

Will Bullas Store

Operating System

ADMINISTRATIVE POLICIES

Receiving Orders

Transactions at the Will Bullas store will be done in a very simple, yet effective manner. In the store there will be a counter with a cash drawer. All sales will be written up on a sales ticket using a cost mark to label the items sold. Cash transactions will be the simplest and most straight forward. Customers wishing to pay with check must have California checks and identification. Visa, Mastercard, and American Express are exceptable credit cards but must be verified with the use of a Zon.

For sales documents, see Appendix C.

Paying the Suppliers

The suppliers will be paid under terms of net 30. Large orders such as beginning inventory in year 1 and additional needed inventory in year 4 will be paid C.O.D. All quantity discounts will be taken.

Reporting to Management

Because the management team consists of the CEO, sales manager, and Board of Directors, there will be excellent communication through the corporation. Board meetings and meeting between the CEO and sales manager are the methods to achieve this communication and shall be held monthly and weekly respectively. Documents needed for these meetings are monthly sales goal sheets, cash flow statements, profit and loss statements and balance sheet.

Employee Training

The CEO is responsible for training the sales manager in the areas of product knowledge, sales, inventory control, and various duties related to the position. An employee manual is in development stages to include all information relating to the store and the responsibilities of each employee.

Dolores and Sixth
Carmel-by-the-Sea
(408) 649-0688

Will Bullas Store

Operating System

Employee Incentive Plan

A Sales Bonus Incentive will be used encorage high sales to achieve the projected monthly sales as well as to drive the profit of the corporation. When the set monthly goal is met, the store manager has earned a bonus. The amount of the bonus is determined by the a) the difference in actual monthly sales to projected sales b) the percentage of sales the store manager was responsible for. The amount of the bonus for the store manager once the goal is reached will range from $100 to $500.

Inventory Control

Inventory will be tracked by using a cost mark system. Under this type of coding a large T-shirt that costs $30 would be marked: **NOTSL**
Inventory sold will be recorded nightly with use of computer and inventory will be taken as needed to check sales projections of beginning and ending inventory as well as for ordering additional supply.

Returns

Returns will be made for customers with a sales receipt. Cases for returns will be handled on an individual basis. Exchanges for different merchandise can usually be arranged.

Budgets

Company budgets for all expense items will be monitored by the CEO and overseen by the Board of Directors. Travel, phone usage, car allowances, entertainment and other expense items may only be used for company related activities by the CEO, store manager, or Board of Directors. It is the responsiblity of the CEO to make sure these expenses do not exceed the amount budgeted for each account. If an expense is underestimated for the month, there needs to be notification to the Board and adjustment to the estimated monthly cash flow.

Dolores and Sixth
Carmel-by-the-Sea
(408) 649-0688

Will Bullas Store

Operating System

Security Systems

Customer lists will be protected by the computer's database to be accessed by the CEO and Secretary of the Board. Cash will be secured through daily deposits in addition to keeping less than $200 in the cash drawer overnight. Trade secrets will be kept within the organization through the use of a Non Compete Agreement, Appendix K.

Documents

Sales tickets, order forms, credit card authorization forms, monthly sales goal sheets, daily transaction and deposit sheets are included in Appendix C.

Planning Chart

	1992							1993			
Activity	May	June	July	Aug	Sept	Oct	Nov	Dec	Jan	Feb	Mar	Apr
FACILITY												
Lease Negotiations		—	—	→								
Sign Lease				—	→							
Renovation and Design					—	—	→					
Order Store Supplies					—	→						
MERCHANDISE												
Find Licensees		—	→									
Preview Designs			—	→								
Begin Ordering					—	→						
Confirm Orders						—	→					
Check in Inventory						—	—	→				
Price Inventory							—	—	→			
Stock Store								—	—	→		
EMPLOYEES												
Interview					—	→						
Hire						—	—	→				
Begin Training							—	—	→			
Positions Starts								—	—	→		
MISCELLANEOUS												
Pre-opening promo/Advertising								—	—	→		
Grand Opening									—	→		
CORPORATION												
Filing Articles of Incorporation		—	→									
Preparing the Corporation's ByLaws		—	—	→								
Finish Corporation Process				—	—	→						

Will Bullas Store

Operating System

RISK ANALYSIS

Sales Projections

If sales projections prove wrong we will take immediate steps to evaluate the cash flows, cut expenses and propose a new adjusted projection for sales.

Competition

There is much competition within the area of Carmel-by-the-Sea because of the nature of the tourist town, lots of art and t-shirt shops. If these competitors made an attempt to destroy our marketplace or initiate a price war, we would take the following actions:
- Emphasize uniqueness though advertising and promotions.
- Lower prices to comparable price of competitor's items.
- Negotiations with competition.

Labor

This is not a labor intensive business however, we do need experienced and responsible sales people. If needed labor is unavailable, we would look to family members to employ temporarily until necessary employees are found.

Supply

If supply deficiencies develop we would look to:

- Finding new licensees
- Using manufactured products and adding art or logo

Dolores and Sixth
Carmel-by-the-Sea
(408) 649-0688

Will Bullas Store

Operating System

Capital

If needed capital is unobtainable, the Will Bullas Store, Inc. would consider using debt to leverage the start-up. The most propable solution would be to have an investor sign for a line of credit with a bank, making the investor both a shareholder and menber of the Board.

Product Liability

The General Business Policy through Farmer's Insurance Group will cover liabilities up to $1,000,000 , fire and water damage of shell including inventory, and business interuption.

Management Problems

If problems with management were to arise, the corporation would need to access the problem and determine a solution. Steps to be taken would include warning, probation period, or termination.

Delayed Product Development

If setting up licensees takes longer than anticipated, product development will also be delayed. If this happens we will have to concentrate on getting the production underway of priority products. In addition we could add products that would have a shorter production time. Using already produced items and then characterizing them with Will Bullas art or insignia is also a viable option.

Dolores and Sixth
Carmel-by-the-Sea
(408) 649-0688

Will Bullas Store

Operating System

SALVAGING ASSETS

If any of the risks on the previous two pages do materialize and make this venture unsuccessful, we needed to be prepared to pay back investors and any creditors. This would have to be accomplished by salvaging assets. The following assets could be salvaged:

- Inventory
- Computer and software
- Store fixtures
- Store furniture

Growth Plan

Will Bullas Store

Growth Plan

NEW OFFERING TO MARKET

In the future the Will Bullas, Inc. would like to expand the retail division of the Will Bullas Stores in various ways:

New Locations

San Francisco
Laguna Beach
La Jolla

There are many ideal locations for a Will Bullas Store. Laguna Beach, La Jolla, and San Francisco would be good locations because each attract thousands of tourists as well as having a large resident community. Expanding out of California, locations such as Aspen, Colorado would be an option in the future.

Distribution Centers

We would very much like to see Will Bullas designs and products in various distribution centers such as Hallmark and other gift stores, and in department stores. A small gallery set up could be very effective in these types of stores. Distribution to these stores could be pursued by the both licensees and the Will Bullas, Inc. to assure quality presentation.

Franchise

Will Bullas Store, Inc. will reserve the right to franchise the Will Bullas Store in the future. Franchising would allow for expansion to several states with the capital requirements paid by franchisees.

Dolores and Sixth
Carmel-by-the-Sea
(408) 649-0688

Will Bullas Store

Growth Plan

Projected Revenues

Store location	Projected Revenues
San Francisco	$500,000 first year
Laguna Beach	$400,000 first year
La Jolla	$400,000 first year

Capital Requirements

Capital Needed	Financial Requirements
Inventory	$70,000 start-up
Capital Expenditures	
Renovation	$20,000 to $40,000 range
Computer	$3000
Lease	$25,000 and above
Advertising	$10,000 per year
General/ Admin. Costs	$60,000 to $90,000 range

Dolores and Sixth
Carmel-by-the-Sea
(408) 649-0688

Will Bullas Store

Growth Plan

Personnel Requirements

As additional stores are added, we will need to hire personnel for management and sales for the individual stores. The positions to be added are full-time store manager and one to three part-time sales people for each additional store. Furthermore, a buyer and marketing assistant will need to be added to the management team once the retail division has expanded to three or more stores.

Job Title	Salary	Description
Store Manager	$24,000	Responsible for all store activities and managerial responsibilities including: • Training new employees • Sales • Inventory Control • Weekly reports to CEO
Part-time Sales People	$8 per hour	Sales is primary responsibility
Buyer	$28,000	Negotiation and purchase of inventory for all stores
Marketing Assistant	$26,000	Responsible for all retail advertising and promotions.

Dolores and Sixth
Carmel-by-the-Sea
(408) 649-0688

Will Bullas Store

Growth Plan

EXIT STRATEGY

The success of our expansion efforts and our ability to capture the market will greatly influence our exit strategy. Depending upon the agreement of the investors, Board of Directors, and other involved parties we can plan an exit in ten to fifteen years. By then, we feel we will have expanded the retail division to its most profitable potential. At the present time, we anticipate the following options for exit strategies:

Merge with a public company

Franchise Will Bullas Stores

Public Offering as subsidiary to Will Bullas, Inc.

Will Bullas Store

Appendix
Table of Contents

Resume	A
Shareholders Agreement	B
Sales Documents	C
By Laws and Articles of Incorporation	D
Future Products	E
Tourist Magazine Cover	F
Press Release	G
Sample Advertisements	H
Five Year Sales and Graph	I
Inventory Turnover Ratios	J
Non-Compete Agreement	K
Employment Contract	L
Confidentiality Statement	M
Population Trends	N

CHAPTER 3
SIEMPRE ENVISIONS

Written by:
    Catherine Hawthorne

Computer hardware:
    Apple Macintosh

Computer software:
    Microsoft Word

Printing:
    Signal Graphics

Book used to write business plan :
    The Entrepreneur's Planning Handbook

Overview

The Institute for Entrepreneurship and Creativity at Metropolitan State College of Denver was started in 1986 to offer a full range of academic courses, forums with national and local business leaders, and seminars for business professions. It was the first program of its kind in the Rocky Mountain region and presents a unique learning experience that extends beyond the traditional classroom approach.

Students interested in entrepreneurship can obtain a Bachelors of Science degree in management with an emphasis in managerial entrepreneurship through the School of Business. The Contract Major Program at the college allows students to incorporate entrepreneurship classes in a self-designed degree program. Entrepreneurial Business Planning is the last course students take during their senior year before graduation. In this class, students are required to write individual business plans on a venture they plan on starting after graduation.

Cathy Hawthorne was a student in the entrepreneurship program and wanted to start a graphic design business as a home-based business and then expand it to a retail location. She wrote her business plan on Siempre Envisions and used the suggested format and subtitles found in The Entrepreneur's Planning Handbook. Her business plan is an excellent example of a home-based service business that could be started with little capital, which is typical of many businesses started by FastTrac graduates.

Siempre Envisions was included in this book because it is clearly written, and easy to read and follow. Cathy incorporated graphic designs into her plan. They illustrate how a few engaging designs and simple graphics on each page can improve the attractiveness and readability of a business plan. This sample shows how writing a business plan, on a computer can enhance the presentation of vital information presented in the plan.

Cathy used many bullets to summarize key points but, she could have used more charts to display information that appeared in text form. A weakness of the business plan was splitting the figures on each financial statement on two separate pages. These figures should have been combined and reformatted so each financial statement was on one page. Review Cathy's growth plan since it is an excellent example of how to write this section of your plan.

Because her venture required little investment and her business plan proved it could be profitable, Catherine launched this business after graduation and hopes to achieve the goals she outlined in her business plan. She was able to keep her expenses to a minimum by subcontracting work she could not perform herself.

Review her business plan and use it as a guide in preparing a business plan for any service business. The authors of Sample Business Plans want to thank Cathy for allowing us to include her plan in this book.

BUSINESS PLAN CRITIQUE

Name: Siempre Envisions

I. Overall Appearance and Format

Strength:

The writer effectively uses subtitles and bullets throughout the business plan. Each page has a good balance of white space, making it attractive to the eye and easy to read. The plan is 46 pages long, which is a good length for this type of business. Title pages for each section in the business plan are attractively designed to divide each of the major sections in the business plan.

Weakness:

Charts and graphs are not used, which could have enhanced some of the sections.

II. Cover Page

Strength:

The writer includes the contact name, address, and telephone number along with a graphic symbol for the company.

III. Table of Contents

Strength:

The writer includes subtitles in the Table of Contents, which allows the reader to quickly locate desired information. The Table of Contents also lists the page numbers for each section in the Appendix.

IV. Executive Summary

Weakness:

This section is not written in letter form and addressed to the reader. It fails to mention the competition for this business.

BUSINESS PLAN CRITIQUE

V. Management and Organization

Strength:

The writer includes all the subtitles for this section adequately.

Weakness:

The writer could have listed the Advisory Council in chart form and included their expertise and responsibilities.

Insurance

This subhead refers to obtaining life insurance for the entrepreneur and key management team to fund the buy-sell agreement, not product liability which this writer describes.

VI. Product/Service

Strength:

Purpose of the Business

This section is written clearly so the reader understands the purpose of the business.

Weakness:

Trademarks and Copyrights

The writer addresses how the company will obtain trademarks and copyrights for the customers instead of explaining how this business will protect its intellectual property. This discussion of special services the company offers should have been placed under the Unique Features subhead in the product service plan.

Product Liability

This section should have included what insurance coverage is necessary for the company to protect against any liability.

BUSINESS PLAN CRITIQUE

VII. Marketing Plan

Strength:

The industry study is done well and factual so the reader can easily understand the present and future economic trends of the industry. The competitive matrix chart is well laid out and contains all pertinent information.

Weakness:

<u>Target Market Profile</u>

This section should provide a list of potential customers by the company's name, address, telephone number, and the contact person.

<u>Market Penetration</u>

The writer does not include any innovative ways to contact potential customers. This makes it obvious to the reader that not much thought or time was devoted to preparing the information in this subsection.

VIII. Financial Plan

Strength:

<u>Assumptions</u>

The assumptions are numbered and correspond with the Cash Flow chart of accounts. The writer uses new assumptions for every year of Cash Flow. This shows that she understands how various aspects of her business will change over time.

Weakness:

Cash Flow monthly figures are split on two pages and should appear on one page. Cash Flow proformas for year two and three should also be on one page. The Income Statement and Balance Sheets for years one, two, and three should likewise be on one page.

The financial documents should not have taken more than about six pages of the business plan instead of 14 pages.

BUSINESS PLAN CRITIQUE

IX. Operating System

Strength:

<u>Administrative Policies and Procedures</u>

This is a well-written section and indicates that the writer understands all the daily operations of the business.

<u>Risk Analysis and Alternative Plans of Action</u>

The writer does not address all of the risks inherent in the business. This shows that the entrepreneur has not considered all the possible problems that could be encountered as the business grows.

X. Growth Plan

Strength:

The writer addresses all the important information that should be included in a growth plan. This is one of the strongest sections in the business plan.

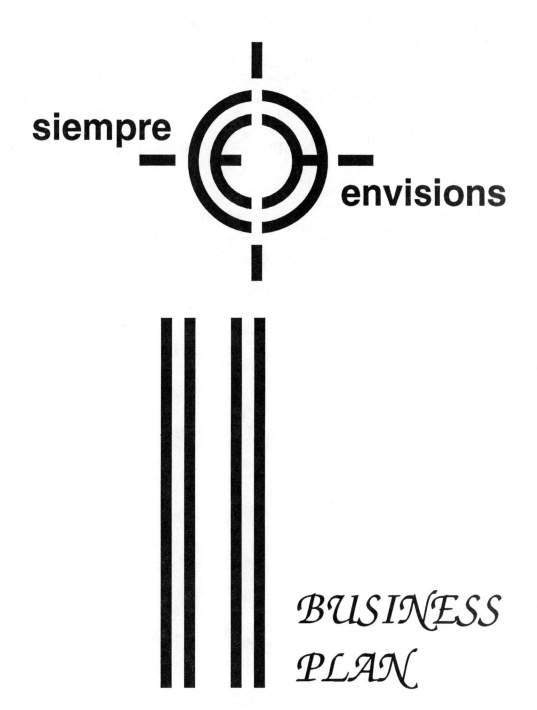

Business Plan
for

Siempre Envisions

Prepared for

Dr. Courtney Price
MGT442 - Entrepreneurial Business Planning
Metropolitan State College of Denver

© Spring, 1992

by
Catherine Hawthorne

Table of Contents

Executive Summary ....

Management and Organization ....
    Management Team ....
    Compensation ....
    Contract Agreement ....
    Advisory Council ....
    Infrastructure ....
    Insurance ....
    Functional Organization Chart ....

Service Plan ....
    Purpose of the Service ....
    Unique Features ....
    Stage of Development ....
    Trademarks and Copyrights ....
    Product Liability ....
    Related Services and Spin-offs ....
    Production ....
    Environmental Factors ....

Marketing Plan ....
    Industry Profile ....
    Competition Profile ....
    Customer Profile ....
    Target Market Profile ....
    Market Penetration ....
    Advertising and Promotion ....
    Trade Shows ....
    Future Markets ....
    Pricing Profile ....
    Gross Margin on Products ....

Financial Plan ....
    Assumptions ....
    Cash Flow Projection - January - June, 1992..
    Cash Flow Projection - July - December, 1992..
    Cash Flow Projection - 1993...
    Cash Flow Projection - 1994...
    Profit and Loss Statement - 1992...
    Profit and Loss Statement - 1993...
    Profit and Loss Statement - 1994...
    Balance Sheet - 1992 ....
    Balance Sheet - 1993 ....
    Balance Sheet - 1994 ....

Operating and Control System ....
    Administrative Policies and Procedures..
    Administrative Controls ....
    Documents and Paper Flow ....
    Risk Analysis and Alternative Plans of Action..
    Salvaging Assets..

Growth Plan...
    New Offerings to Market ....
    Capital Requirements ....
    Personnel Requirements ....
    Exit Strategy ....

Appendices
    A- Resume of Catherine Hawthorne
    B- Contract Agreement
    C- Intellectual and Artistic Property Agreement
    D- Promotional Literature

List of Charts of Graphs

Functional Organization Chart ....
Competitive Matrix Chart..
Planning Chart...
New Offerings Chart ....

Summary and Executive Overview

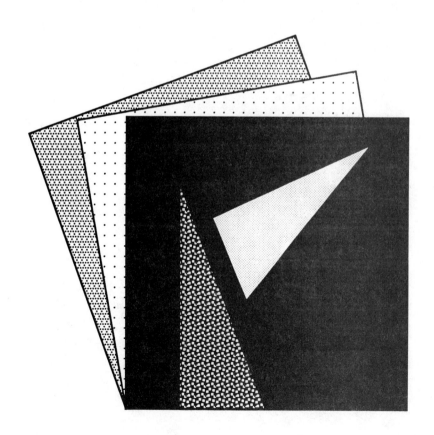

Executive Summary

Siempre Envisions, located in Denver, Colorado, designs graphics and technical documentation to enhance customers' image building and publishing efforts. The marketing focus is on high technology businesses in the Denver metropolitan area who have a need for quality, affordable graphics and technical design.

Siempre Envisions operates as a part-time, home-based business. A Macintosh computer with graphics and desktop publishing software is available to meet the needs of the clients. Contracting with outside service bureaus for high-quality imaging and printing is offered.

Siempre Envisions staff accommodates businesses who require freelance professional graphic and technical designers to work with their "in-house" team as well as those clients who have no internal graphic support.

The target market will consist of medical and computer manufacturers, publishers, research and development companies, engineering consulting firms, and software designers.

Catherine Hawthorne, sole proprietor of Siempre Envisions, has several years experience in the graphics, printing, publishing and engineering fields and has worked extensively in presentation graphics, desktop publishing, technical illustration and documentation. Her contribution to the business will be that of graphic designer and executive director.

Incorporation of Siempre Envisions is planned for January, 1994. The corporation, consisting of the executive director, a production artist, a marketing administrator, a graphic designer and an administrative assistant will be fully operational by February, 1995.

An injection of capital will be needed in late 1993 in order to accomplish the growth goals of the business. At that time, a small business loan from a banker or other lender will be sought.

Management
and
Organization

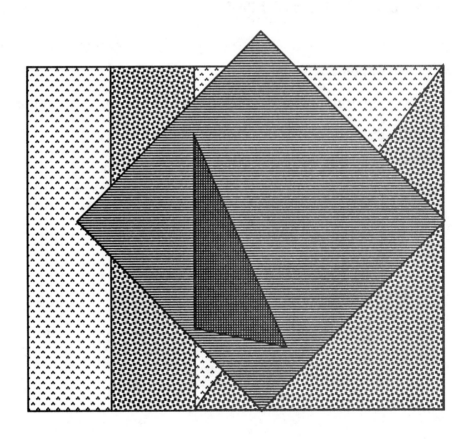

Management and Organization

Siempre Envisions, of Denver, Colorado, designs graphics and technical documents for new and expanding high-technology businesses. This service focuses on companies who have a need for freelance professionals to help enhance their image building, documentation and presentation efforts.

Catherine Hawthorne, sole proprietor, is currently operating Siempre Envisions as a part-time home-based business with the assistance of a contracted desktop publishing specialist. Siempre Envisions plans to incorporate in January, 1994, and have a full-time staff of five by the end of 1995.

♦ **Management Team**

Siempre Envisions management team (outlined in the Functional Organization Chart at the end of this section) will consist of:

- Executive Director - Catherine Hawthorne
- Production Artist
- Marketing Administrator
- Graphic Designer
- Administrative Assistant

Catherine Hawthorne has several years experience in the graphics, printing and publishing industry and has worked extensively in presentation graphics, promotional graphics, layout and pasteup, typesetting, desktop publishing, computer graphics, illustration, and advertising layout. (Please see detailed resume in Appendix A.)

Her initial contribution to Siempre Envisions will be that of graphic designer and production artist. She is a skilled computer operator, and will use the Macintosh personal computer system to create logos, letterhead design, promotional literature, annual reports, newsletters, presentations, graphics, typography and drawings.

A production artist will be contracted in the June, 1992 to assist in the creation, production, and coordination of promotional marketing materials. This qualified candidate will have a minimum of 3 years desktop publishing experience working on Macintosh personal computers, familiarity with graphic design capabilities, proficiency on Quark XPress and Aldus FreeHand or Adobe Illustrator. This position will be permanently filled in July, 1994.

The marketing administrator will develop marketing strategies, perform market planning and analysis and coordinate outside sales. A qualified candidate will have a B.A./M.B.A. and a minimum of 6 years experience in marketing/sales of print media. The ability to interact with technical and scientific customers, as well as exhibiting strong organizational skills, is essential. This person will be on board in February, 1995.

The graphic designer position requires excellent board production skills, understanding of 4-color graphics, and advanced Macintosh ability using Quark Xpress and FreeHand software. A qualified candidate must have the capability of creating high quality design and production in a fast-paced environment. Excellent written communication skills are required. Promotional and/or technical copywriting helpful. Degree in graphic design or related field a plus. This position will be filled in September, 1995.

The administrative assistant will provide administrative and clerical support to the CEO and Marketing Department. This individual should have excellent typing, proofreading and written communication skills. Knowledge of Microsoft Word and Excel is necessary. Experience in printing and publishing is helpful. This person will be hired in March, 1994.

♦ **Compensation**

Siempre Envisions will begin operation as a sole proprietorship, using contract workers and temporaries on an "as-needed" basis. A mutually-agreed upon hourly rate will be established with each contractor. As sole proprietor, Catherine Hawthorne will receive all cash profits made by the business.

Upon incorporation, Siempre Envisions will offer each employee a salary, workman's compensation, and a corporate benefits package which includes two weeks annual vacation and a employee-funded retirement plan.

All employees will be either exempt or non-exempt. Salaries and wages will be commensurate with experience and the market. Cost-of-living increases will be evaluated annually on the employee's anniversary. Cash bonuses, from corporate profits, will be considered and may be rewarded to employees.

- **Contract Agreement**

    All contract workers will be required to sign a Contract Agreement (see Appendix B) with Siempre Envisions. Hourly rates will be in writing and re-negotiated annually with each contractor - commencing January 1st and ending December 31st. On the last day of the month, each contractor will be required to submit an invoice for the hours worked during that month.

- **Advisory Council**

    Members of the advisory council will consist of a small retail business owner, an attorney specializing in small business, a computer software consultant and an advertising executive. Siempre Envisions will hold quarterly meetings with the advisory board, and at that time will issue a progress and financial report.

- **Infrastructure**

    Members of the infrastructure are:
    - Accountant
    - Bookkeeper
    - Copyright Lawyer

- **Insurance**

    Siempre Envisions will have renter's insurance to cover personal property. In addition, we will carry property liability insurance with limits of $150,000 for individuals. Meetings with customers will be done at their place of business in order to protect against lawsuits incurred by accidents or harm to customers at the residence of Catherine Hawthorne.

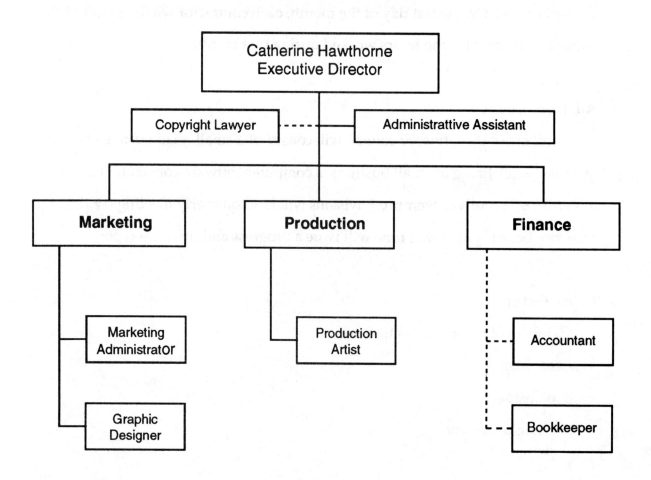

Service Plan

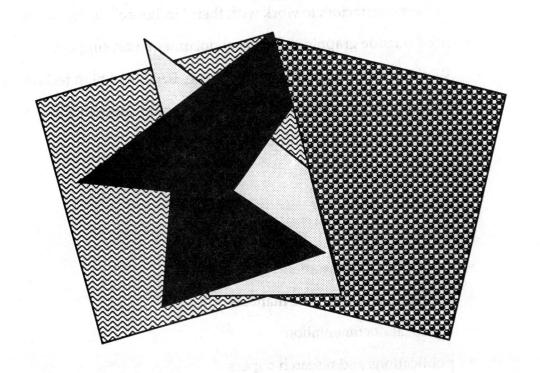

Service Plan

♦ **Purpose of the Service**

Siempre Envisions designs graphics and technical documents to help customers enhance their image building and publishing efforts. The focus is on high-technology companies who have a need for quality, affordable graphics and technical documentation from freelance professionals.

♦ **Unique Features**

Staff accommodates businesses who:
- require contractors to work with their "in-house" design team
- need outside graphic or technical documentation support

Working knowledge of manufacturing, R&D, and high technology company operations and planning is furnished. "One-stop shopping" is offered for both general business and technical services:
- logo design
- corporate newsletter
- annual reports
- promotional literature
- operation and reference manuals
- technical documentation
- publications and research papers
- CAD and engineering drawings

Assistance and contribution is offered in preparing:

- slide presentations
- exhibits, conferences and trade shows

♦ **Stage of Development**

Siempre Envisions is operating as a part-time, home-based business, and presently has three clients on a long-term contract basis. A Macintosh computer with graphics and desktop publishing software is available to meet customers needs. Outside service bureaus are used for high-quality imaging and printing.

♦ **Trademarks and Copyrights**

Siempre Envisions offers creation of logos, servicemarks and trademarks for corporations. Performing research and filing for copyright or trademark registration is available at the client's request.

The Intellectual and Artistic Property Agreement (see Appendix C) will be adhered to unless otherwise agreed to in writing.

◆ **Product Liability**

Siempre Envisions guarantees delivery of finished "camera ready" artwork. All work requests must be accompanied by a written purchase order. In a case where the client delays a job request for 30 or more days, Siempre Envisions reserves the right to cancel order with a 30-days written notice.

Responsibility is assumed for printing quality, costs incurred for typographical and pasteup errors made to final graphic layout, and damages or loss of original art until delivery is signed for by the customer. Content and format changes made by the client to final artwork will be billed additionally to the customer at rate of $30 per hour.

◆ **Related Services and Spin-offs**

In the computer graphics, promotion and advertising area there are many avenues that Siempre Envisions could venture along:

- mixed-media arts
- technical illustration
- information and educational graphics
- animation
- 3-D and video production

Another spin-off would be graphic support:

- developing graphic software packages
- training facilities
- exhibits, trade shows and workshops

As in any venture, spin-offs are limited by manpower, innovation, expertise and funding. Expanding into other art forms and computer technologies by late 1995 may by explored with other companies or individuals.

◆ **Production**

All graphic design, documentation, and desktop publishing will be home-based, until such time that deadlines and work load require subcontracting to outside production artists. All printing and high-quality graphic output will be performed by outside service bureaus and subcontractors. All document printing will be performed by a local print shop. Prior to moving to an office building location in early 1994, a decision to bring laser printing, image setting and pre-press setup in-house may be addressed.

◆ **Environmental Factors**
- participate in local recycling programs
- volunteered time and service for community awareness of Earth Day 1970 in California and Earth Day 1990 in Denver, Colorado
- rewarded for work on several renewable and solar energy design publications and exhibits with local engineers and scientists
- initiated white paper recycling
- encourage clients to use recycled paper for printed material
- initiated contract with an outside silver recovery vendor for film pickup

All computer workstations are ergonomically designed to adapt to the operator. Chair height, computer screen height, keyboard height and tilt are flexible and can be adjusted for individual comfort.

Siempre Envisions offers a smoke-free office environment

Marketing Plan

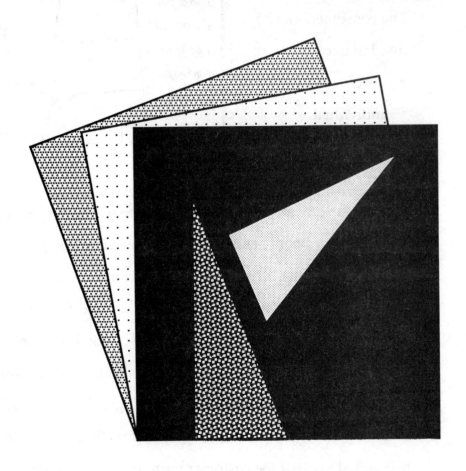

Marketing Plan

- **Industry Profile**

    Computer-generated graphics and publishing began escalating in 1987 and has been growing ever since (Presentation Products, March, 1990). Desktop publishing, presentation art, and computer graphics are the primary tools Siempre Envisions will use to penetrate the visual material market, so it is important to understand this medium. The consumers can be divided into:

    - corporate
    - individual
    - non-profit
    - art collector

    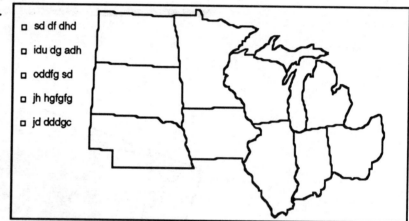

    Siempre Envisions' initial focus will be on the high-end technology community. The computer boom has had a positive effect on computer graphics. As more people become "computer literate" they also become aware of the advantages of using computers to perform design functions (i.e, modifying, storing, adding and deleting data). Competent computer operators also soon learn their specialties and personal limitations. In theory, this should create a magnetism between the educated customers and the professional computer graphics artist. After years of training, schooling and experience in the graphic arts field, the designer becomes the person best suited to assist the customer with promotion, design and documentation.

◆ ◆ ◆

Macworld, April, 1992, printed a review of their annual selection of the best art the "Mac" has to offer in the 1991 Macintosh Masters Showcase. Graphic designers exhibited a broad range of what computer art currently has to offer.

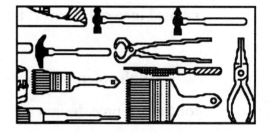

"...from intricate and precise graphic designs and technical illustration, to alternative realities simulated with 3-D rendering tools..."

Current size – *Presentation Products Magazine*, March, 1990 predicts that desktop presentations market to reach nearly $9 billion by 1993.

"The worldwide market for hardware, software and supplies for desktop presentations will grow to more than $8.9 billion by 1993, up from $4.0 billion in 1989."

Looking at this demand for continually improving software indicates that more and more graphic designers are using computers as design media and are demanding "the best tools" from software packages. Graphic output is high resolution and professional-looking – creating end-user demand for high-quality, affordable graphics in a very short turn-around time. Speed and quality will be the factors for success or failure of graphic designers and desktop publishers in the 1990s.

Not to be misleading, much of the multi-media computer art is very costly – requiring editing, music scores and audio/video mixing, but Siempre Envisions' focus is not in that arena. The late 20th century has been called the "Information Age", and one of the main ways to get the information disseminated is through printed material. This is Siempre Envisions primary media.

Growth potential – work for the freelance artist is inversely related to work for the full-time designer. Employee layoffs and company personnel hiring freezes in the early 1990s in the United States has created a demand for freelance graphic designers and desktop publishers to get the jobs done. Companies have more work than their staff can handle so, historically, they contract with free-lancers on a temporary to long-term basis. Growth will flatten out as the economy picks up – however, the astute designer has used the downturn as a way to infiltrate an extremely competitive market and could quite possibly become an invaluable contractor.

One factor limiting the growth of the print media would be an accelerated demand for video or broadcast media. In the early 1990s, technological costs continue to dictate production – and print media is still the best buy on a cost per thousand basis. (<u>Contemporary Advertising</u>, C. Bovee and W. Arens, 1989.)

Industry trends – reported average profitability for graphic design: return on sales - 6.5%; return on assets -14.7%; return on net worth - 28.3% (<u>Industry Norms and Key Business Ratios</u>, 1991). This area includes, to name of few, desktop publishing, illustration, games, educational and mapping applications, movies, and editors. Some of these areas are rapidly expanding (i.e., mapping and games) and some have lagged in new technological changes. Desktop publishing and graphic arts are areas considered to be "low-key" in 1992, with most product development focusing on updating existing software for enhanced user ability (*Macworld*, April, 1992) rather than new technology. These trends indicate Siempre Envisions could save the expense of purchasing new software for the business.

Seasonality factors – most brochures, and documentation are created after the first quarter to the year – from March through August. Conferences and workshops are often scheduled during the off-season (or off-peak) times of the year and slide presentations, poster sessions and exhibits are prepared in February, and July through September. The "downtime" for Siempre Envisions would be Thanksgiving through the middle of February when work often slows to a halt during the holiday season.

♦ Competition Profile

Siempre Envisions' competition are those businesses who have engineering and scientific publishing and presentation experience.
- graphic designers
- typesetters and lithographers
- print shops and publishers

Competitive Matrix Chart for Graphic Designer and Desktop Publishing

Company	Price	Quality	Unique Features	Marketing/ Advertising	Geographic Location	Strengths/ Weaknesses
Siempre Envisions	3	High Accurate	Creative, Innovative, Technical	Word-of mouth	S.E. Denver	Fast, Part-time, Excellence
Signal Graphics	2	Average	Copying, Printing	Coupons Direct Mail	S.E. Denver	Fast, Inexpensive
Core Graphics	1	Below Average	Design, Printing	Coupons Direct Mail	Englewood	Print shop
Johnson Printing	4	High	Publishing 4-color Imaging, Volume	Catalog Education	Boulder	Reputable, 50 years in business
Alpha Graphics	3	Above Average	Copying Printing On-Site Computer Availability	Franchise Direct sales	Littleton	Helpful, Innovative Print shop
Pollman Marketing	4	Above Average	Marketing, graphics, packaging	Mailer Networking	Boulder	Innovative Design team Largest Competitor

1 = slightly below average
2 = average
3 = slightly above average
4 = above average

◆ **Customer Profile**

   1) primary customers will be:
   - publication services managers
   - documentation support managers
   - engineering staff

   2) secondary customers will be:
   - marketing departments
   - small business owners

◆ **Target Market Profile**

Siempre Envisions will target high-technology businesses in the Denver metropolitan area who have a need for quality, affordable graphics and technical design. The target market will be:
- medical and computer manufacturers
- publishers
- research and development companies
- engineering consulting firms
- software designers

◆ **Market Penetration**

Siempre Envisions will penetrate the high end business and technical market, using word-of-mouth approach. Through referrals, networking and contacts with previous customers and fellow employees, names and addresses of potential new customers and previous clients will be compiled. Each contact will be sent a business card and a pamphlet introducing the business services in:

- logo design
- slide presentations
- product literature
- newsletters
- manuals and brochures
- CAD design
- technical documentation

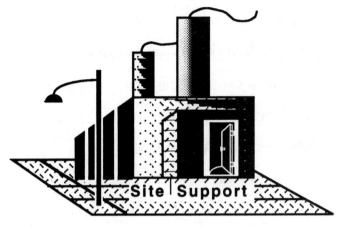

Follow-up within 2 weeks by a telephone call to set a meeting date.

- **Advertising and Promotion**

For the first year, Siempre Envisions will use word-of-mouth advertising by meeting with friends and business associates on a regular basis. Promotion of Siempre Envisions and its business will also be done by attending meetings and networking with metro Denver professional and social organizations – the Denver Advertising Federation and the American Multi-Media Association, Professional Women's organization, Rocky Mountain Inventors and Entrepreneurs Congress, Flying Singles and Up the Creek Ski and Rec Club. In 1994, if the company grows as planned, we research the feasibility of promoting the business card, letterhead and logo design services. Advertising in a local area coupon directory to attract the small retail business owner may be an avenue to use. (See Appendix D - direct mail piece.)

- **Trade Shows**

    A tentative plan is to have a booth at the Denver Advertising show in 1994. This visibility will be used as a communication tool to let the advertising community know Siempre Envisions is doing business. It will also offer the opportunity to network with other designers, photographers, printers and publishers – sharing knowledge, ideas and business strategies.

- **Future Markets**
    - International trade
    - Retired or semi-retired professionals
    - Clubs, non-profit and service organizations - newsletters
    - Mail order catalogs
    - Posters and displays

- **Pricing Profile**
    - Typesetting $12/page (minimum 2 pages)
    - Layout/Graphic Design $20/hour
    - Illustration $23/hour
    - CAD design $25/hour
    - Research and filing $30/hour
    - 35mm slide artwork $10/slide
    - Rush charges (add $10/order)
    - Quantity discounts available
    - Terms: net 30 days, 2%-10 days
    - Senior citizen discounts available

♦ Gross Margin on Products

Siempre Envisions' will generally bid on the total job, however, prices have been established and are competitive with the local printers, typesetters and graphic design businesses. Potential gross profit margins are:

Sales Revenue	Fixed Costs	Net Profit (1 unit)	Net Profit (2 units)	Net Profit (4 units)
Typesetting $12/page	12.00/4=3.00+2.50+4.00= 9.50x2=$19.00-24=$5.00		20%	
	3.00+2.50+4.00=9.50x4= $38.00-48=$10.00			20%
Layout/Design $20/hour	12.00+2.50+4.00=18.50-20=$1.50	7.5%		
	24.00+3.50+4.00=31.50-40=$8.50		21%	
	48.00+4.00+4.00=56.00-80=$24.00			30%
Illustration $23/hour	15.00+2.50+4.00=21.50-23=$1.50	6.5%		
	30.00+3.50+4.00=37.50-46=$8.50		18%	
	60.00+4.00+4.00=68.00-92=$24.00			26%
CAD design $25/hour	15.00+2.50+4.00=21.50-25=$3.50	14%		
	30.00+3.50+4.00=37.50-50=$12.50		25%	
	60.00+4.00+4.00=68.00-100=$32.00			32%
Research $30/hour	18.00+10.00*=$28.00-30=$2.00	6%		
	36.00+10.00*=$46.00-60=$14.00		23%	
	72.00+10.00*=$82.00-120=$38			32%
35mm slides $10/slide	$12/6=2.00+2.50+4.00= $8.50-10=$1.50	15%		

* mileage, transportation, parking, etc.

Fixed costs:
    $ 12.00/hr   labor (type, design)
    $ 15.00/hr   labor (illustration, CAD)
    $ 18.00/hr   labor (research)
    $ 2.50   facility (including utilities)
    $ 4.00   office overhead

*Financial
Plan*

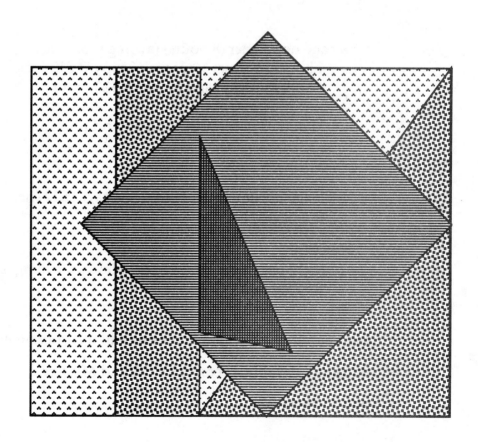

Financial Plan

- **Assumptions**

    Sales – Siempre Envisions is a part-time home-based business and projects sales at 30-40 hours a month at an average of $22/hour.

    - 4 page brochure (6 hours) (averages $29/hr)

2 hours - typeset 8 pages of copy @ $12/page	$96
4 hours - design and layout @ $20/hour	80
	176
Materials (laser prints, supplies and output)	24
	$200

    - 6 page newsletter (8 hours) (averages $25/hr)

4 hours - typeset 10 pages of copy @ $12/page	$120
4 hours - design and layout @ $20/hour	80
	200
Materials (laser prints, clipart and photos)	40
	$240

    - 100 page document (25 hours) (averages $12/hr)

@ 4 pages/hour	$300

    - 2 - 11x17 page CAD drawings (14 hours) (averages $25/hr)

@ $25/hour	$350

    Incorporation – Siempre Envisions will incorporate in January, 1994.

    Accounts Payable – Personal VISA and Mastercard credit card charge, payable in 30 days.

◆ ◆ ◆

Accounts Receivable – Terms are payment due upon receipt of work. For pre-approved credit customers, terms are 2%10, net 30 days.

Start-up Costs – include purchase or a Macintosh LC computer, printer, phone, office desk and chair totalling $3300.00 at 10% financing.

Income Tax – income tax rate for Siempre Envisions is 34%.

◆ ◆ ◆

- **Cash Flow Projection – January - June, 1992**

Income	Note	Jan	Feb	Mar	Apr	May	June
Sales ($)	1		200	200	800	400	400
Cash with Order	2				200		
Received on Account	3			400		800	600
<u>Total Monthly</u>				<u>400</u>	<u>200</u>	<u>800</u>	<u>600</u>
<u>Cumulative Cash</u>				<u>400</u>	<u>600</u>	<u>1400</u>	<u>2000</u>
Outgo							
Purchases	4				500		
Equipment	5	100	100	100	100	100	100
Rent	6	140	140	140	140	140	140
Contract Workers	7					100	
Supplies	8	50		50	30	90	25
Auto	9	60	70	60	30	40	40
Telephone	10	10	15	20	10	10	40
Power & Gas	11	5	5	5	4	3	3
Renters Insurance	12	10	10	10	10	10	10
Loans to Self	13		400	400	400	400	400
Marketing	14	50					
Advertising	15						70
Miscellaneous	16	30	25	25	30	35	25
<u>Total Monthly Outgo</u>		<u>455</u>	<u>765</u>	<u>810</u>	<u>1154</u>	<u>928</u>	<u>853</u>
<u>Cumulative Outgo</u>		<u>455</u>	<u>1220</u>	<u>2030</u>	<u>3184</u>	<u>4112</u>	<u>4965</u>
<u>Cum. Cash - Outgo</u>		<u>-455</u>	<u>-1220</u>	<u>-1630</u>	<u>-2584</u>	<u>-2712</u>	<u>-2965</u>

Footnotes on Cash Flow
1. Sales projections based on seasonality.
   Average 1st quarter =9 hrs/mo.; average 2nd quarter = 24 hrs/mo.
2. Cash on retainer.
3. Terms of invoice - 2%10, net 30.
4. Purchase of software packages.
5. Negotiated an 18-month personal loan agreement - 10% interest.
6. Rent is calculated at 20% of home sq. ft.
7. Additional manpower will be required to complete order.
8. Cost for initial graphic supplies. Bulk supplied purchased in May.
9. Auto will be used for customer calling and deliveries.
10. Cash spent for phone charges vary monthly by usage.
11. Cash spent for utilities varies according to season (based on 20% of total electric bill).
12. Semi-yearly payments for liability insurance.
13. Cash paid to owner for services, since business is a sole proprietorship.
14. Initial cost for printing 500 business cards (see Appendix D).
15. Print 200 promotional flyers (see Appendix D).
16. Miscellaneous and emergency expenses not previously in budget.

♦ Cash Flow Projection – July - December, 1992

Income	Note	Jul	Aug	Sep	Oct	Nov	Dec
Sales ($)	1	800	1000	2000	1000	500	200
Cash with Order	2	200	200	500			
Received on Account	3	200	700	1700	800	1000	50
Total Monthly		400	900	2200	800	1000	50
Cumulative Cash		2400	3300	5500	6300	7300	7350

Outgo	Note	Jul	Aug	Sep	Oct	Nov	Dec
Purchases	4		300				
Equipment	5	100	100	100	100	100	100
Rent	6	140	140	140	140	140	140
Contract Workers	7		150	200			
Supplies	8	20	90	90	10	20	5
Auto	9	60	70	60	30	20	20
Telephone	10	10	15	20	25	10	10
Power & Gas	11	3	3	3	4	5	5
Renter's Insurance	12	10	10	10	10	10	10
Loans to Self	13	400	400	400	400	400	400
Marketing	14	50					
Advertising	15		45				
Miscellaneous	16	40	35	45	30	15	35
Total Monthly Outgo		833	1358	1068	749	720	725
Cumulative Outgo		5798	7156	8224	8973	9693	10418
Cum. Cash - Outgo		-3398	-3856	-2724	-2673	-2393	-3068

Footnotes on Cash Flow

1. Sales projections based on seasonality.
   Average 1st quarter =58 hrs/mo.; average 2nd quarter = 27 hrs/mo.
2. Cash on retainer.
3. Terms of invoice.
4. Purchase of software package.
5. Negotiated an 18-month personal loan agreement.
6. Rent is calculated at 20% of home sq. ft.
7. Additional manpower will be required to complete order.
8. Cost for initial graphic supplies. Bulk supplied purchased in Sept.
9. Auto will be used for customer calling and deliveries.
10. Cash spent for phone charges vary monthly by usage.
11. Cash spent for utilities varies according to season (based on 20% of total electric bill).
12. Semi-yearly payments for liability insurance.
13. Cash paid to owner for services, since business is a sole proprietorship.
14. Attend Denver Advertising conference.
15. Direct mail coupon with *The Pocket Coupon Directory* (see Appendix D).
16. Miscellaneous and emergency expenses not previously in budget.

® Cash Flow Projection – 1993

Income	Note	Total
Sales ($)	1	33,400
Cash with Order	2	8,000
Received on Account	3	20,000
Investment	4	10,000
<u>Total Yearly</u>		<u>38,000</u>
<u>Cumulative Cash</u>		<u>45,350</u>

Outgo	Note	Total
Purchases	5	1,300
Equipment	6	600
Sign	7	200
Rent & Lease Dep.	8	3,680
Remodeling/Move	9	1,000
Contract Labor	10	2,400
Consultants	11	3,000
Supplies	12	1,024
Auto	13	1,200
Telephone	14	650
Power & Gas	15	175
Renter's Insurance	16	1,260
License	17	700
Incorporation	18	3,000
Loans to Self	19	10,000
Marketing	20	1,400
Advertising	21	1,200
Miscellaneous	22	900
<u>Total Yearly Outgo</u>		<u>31,889</u>
<u>Cumulative Outgo</u>		<u>42,307</u>
<u>Cum. Cash - Outgo</u>		<u>3,043</u>

Footnotes on Cash Flow

1. Sales projections based on seasonality @ 1600 hours per year.
2. Cash on retainer.
3. Terms of invoice.
4. Small business loan - $10,000 for 1993, $10,000 for 1994 @ 10%.
5. Purchase of expanded memory board and modem.
6. Personal loan paid off in June.
7. Company sign silkscreened in December.
8. Rent is calculated at 20% of home sq. ft. (5% increase), Includes lease deposit on new office space in December.
9. Moving and new office space remodeling expenses in December.
10. Additional manpower required to complete orders.
11. Small business attorney, tax accountant and other professional services.
12. Cost for graphic supplies (5% increase over 1992). Bulk supplies purchased in September.
13. Auto will be used for customer calling and deliveries.
14. Cash spent for phone charges vary monthly by usage. Includes installation of 4 new phone lines with 4 monthly payments (@$100/mo.) beginning December.
15. Cash spent for utilities varies according to season (based on 20% of total electric bill) plus deposit on new office space in December.
16. Renter's insurance paid semi-yearly (includes 5% increase from 1992).
17. Corporate ID, resale license, filing, name search.
18. Miscellaneous expenses for incorporation
19. Cash paid to owner for services through October.
20. General promotion for new business and location.
21. General advertising in yellow pages
22. Miscellaneous and emergency expenses not previously in budget

◆◆◆

- ◆ **Cash Flow Projection – 1994**

Income	Note	Total
Sales ($)	1	136,000
Cash with Order	2	10,000
Received on Account	3	105,000
Investment	4	10,000
<u>Total Yearly</u>		<u>125,000</u>
<u>Cumulative Cash</u>		<u>170,500</u>

Outgo		
Purchases	5	1,000
Equipment	6	12,000
Office Space Lease	7	9,600
Contract Workers	8	1,600
Wages	9	62,000
Payroll Taxes	10	10,800
Supplies	11	1,848
Auto	12	750
Telephone	13	2,400
Power & Gas	14	1,200
Renter's Insurance	15	5,000
Loan Payment	16	6,000
Marketing	17	1,500
Advertising	18	1,000
Miscellaneous	19	2,000
Common Stock	20	1,000
<u>Total Yearly Outgo</u>		<u>119,698</u>
<u>Cumulative Outgo</u>		<u>162,005</u>
<u>Cum. Cash - Outgo</u>		<u>8,495</u>

Footnotes on Cash Flow

1. Sales projections based on seasonality @ 4500 hours.
2. Cash on retainer.
3. Terms of invoice.
4. Small business loan (cash injection for business).
5. Business purchases not previously budgeted for.
6. Furniture and additional computer equipment, laser printer.
7. Office space lease @$800/mo.
8. Summer college intern hired for 3 hours college credit plus $600 stipend. Included other needed contract workers.
9. Wages for administrative assistant (12 mo.), president (12 mo.) and production artist (6 mo.).
10. Payroll taxes include FICA, workers compensation and unemployment taxes.
11. General supplies for operation (includes a 5% increase over 1993 and additional employees).
12. Auto will be used for customer calling.
13. Cash spent for phone charges vary monthly by usage (includes 3 monthly installation charges).
14. Cash spent for utilities varies according to season.
15. Semi-yearly payments.
16. Loan payment to bank @ $600/mo. starts in March.
17. Participate at the Denver Advertising conference, includes booth and exhibitor fees.
18. Yellow pages advertisement. Help wanted ads in classified section of Denver Post.
19. Miscellaneous and petty cash expenses not previously in budget.
20. 40 shares of common stock issued.

◆ Profit and Loss Statement - 1992

Gross Sales		7,500
Less returns and allowances		150
Net sales		7,350
Gross Margin		<u>7,350</u>
Less expenses:		
Administrative expenses	4,400	
Marketing expenses	100	
Financial expenses	5,438	
Inventory	480	
Total expenses		<u>10,418</u>
Net profit before taxes		<u>-3,068</u>
Federal income taxes		-0-
Net profit after taxes		-3,068

♦ Profit and Loss Statement - 1993

Gross Sales		33,400
Less returns and allowances		1,000
Net sales		32,400
Gross Margin		<u>32,400</u>
Less expenses:		
Administrative expenses	10,000	
Marketing expenses	1,500	
Financial expenses	19,389	
Inventory	1,000	
Total expenses		<u>31,889</u>
Net profit before taxes		511
Federal income taxes		184
Net profit after taxes		327

- **Profit and Loss Statement - 1994**

Gross Sales	136,000
Less returns and allowances	2,000
Net sales	134,000
Cost of goods sold	21,600
Gross Margin	<u>112,400</u>
Less expenses:	
Administrative expenses	62,600
Marketing expenses	2,500
Financial expenses	42,798
Inventory	1,800
Total expenses	<u>109,698</u>
Net profit before taxes	2,702
Federal income taxes	405
Net profit after taxes	2,297

♦ **Balance Sheet - 1992**

Assets			Liabilities and Net Worth	
Current asset:			Current liabilities:	
Cash		7,350	Accounts payable	9,218
Accounts Receivable Ret.		150	Short Term Note Payable	1,800
Non-Current Prepaid		600		
Fixed assets				
Equipment	3,300			
Less depreciation	<u>382</u>			
		2,918		
		11,018		**11,018**

♦ **Balance Sheet - 1993**

Assets			Liabilities and Net Worth		
Current asset:			Current liabilities:		
Cash		7,350	Accounts payable	20,089	
Accounts receivable	33,400		Notes payable	600	
Less allowances	-1,000		Interest payable	60	
for doubtful accts		32,400	Taxes payable	184	
Merchandise inventory		100	Wages payable	10,000	
Prepaid expenses		500			30,933
			Long-term liabilities:		
Fixed assets:			Loans payable		10,000
Equipment	4,218				
Less accumulated					
depreciation	-1,792		Net worth:		
		2,426	Retained earnings		3,043
Intangible assets:					
Goodwill		1,200			
		43,976			43,976

- **Balance Sheet - 1994**

Assets			Liabilities and Net Worth		
Current asset:			Current liabilities:		
Cash		45,350	Accounts payable	105,523	
Accounts receivable	136,000		Notes payable	10,000	
Less allowances			Interest payable	1,000	
for doubtful accts	-200	135,800	Taxes payable	3,100	
Merchandise inventory		800	Wages payable	62,000	
Prepaid expenses		1,000			181,623
			Long-term liabilities:		
Fixed assets:			Loans payable		10,000
Equipment	14,426				
Less accumulated			Net worth:		
depreciation	-3,606	10,820	Shares common stock		1,000
			Retained earnings		2,147
Intangible assets:					
Goodwill		1,000			
		194,770			194,770

Operating and Control System

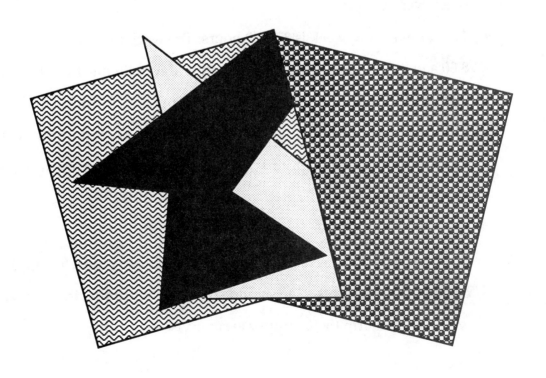

Operating System

- **Administrative Policies and Procedures**
  - Administrative policies and procedures are an attempt to reflect a flexible organization and will be modified as needed to meet current company operating needs. Individual contributions, suggestions, and improvements are encouraged and welcomed.
  - Siempre Envisions is an equal employment opportunity employer and does not discriminate against race, color, sex, creed, political affiliation, martial status or age. It is the company's policy to fill vacancies by promoting from within whenever possible.
  - The normal work week is 37-1/2 hours. The workday is from 8:00 a.m. to 4:30 p.m., Monday through Friday, with one hour for lunch.
  - Siempre Envisions is a task-oriented company and, as such, employees are expected to work the number of hours necessary to get their jobs completed. Employees must obtain prior approval from the appropriate supervisor for overtime requests.

    Absences – Whenever an employee is unable to report for work due to illness or other circumstances s/he should so notify the administrative assistant who will in turn inform the appropriate supervisor.

Pay Periods – Employees will be paid semi-monthly by check on the 15th day and the last day of the month. All contract worker will be paid within 15 days of receipt of invoice.

Time-Off Policy – Full-time employees are allowed a maximum of 22 days time-off during the year. Holidays, vacation, and sick leave are included in this total, allowing the highest amount of individual flexibility. A maximum of 60 hours of leave may be carried forward from one year to the next.

Insurance – No insurance benefits are being offered at this time.

- **Administrative Controls**

    Receiving Orders – All orders will be date stamped and filed as open "work in progress" orders.

    Billing Customers – Pre-approved credit customers will be invoiced upon completion and shipment of the work. Terms: 2%-10 days, net 30. Terms for all other customers: payment due upon receipt of work.
    Siempre Envisions accepts Mastercard and VISA credit cards.

    Collecting Account Receivable – Outstanding invoices will be tracked and a overdue reminder will be send after 30 days. If a billed customer has not paid within 60 days we will use factoring from a financial service company to keep the needed cash flowing into the business.

Inventory Control – Inventory will be kept at a minimum. General office supplies, such as printer paper, envelopes, letterhead, staples, pencils and pens will be purchased in bulk. All graphic supplies will be purchased on an "as needed" basis to complete a job.

- **Documents and Paper Flow**
  - All work requests will be in writing, and mock-ups will be approved by the client prior to beginning the work. The customer will be required to proof a "blue-line" or photo copy before the final artwork will be started.
  - Delays in work schedule will be in writing, and subcontractors will be notified of new schedule completion dates as agreed to in Contractors Agreement, Appendix B.
  - All work in progress will be tracked on a daily basis. A project schedule board will be made up, showing each stage of the project. Completion dates will be assigned to each stage and updated daily.
  - Invoices will be prepared the day the work is complete and will accompany the final artwork.
  - Expense reports will be prepared and submitted to the supervisor on a bi-weekly basis.
  - Deposits to the bank will be done on a daily basis. The administrative assistant will have $50 petty cash for the office, and a running balance will be kept weekly.

Planning Chart

Activity	1993 Oct Nov Dec	1994 Jan Mar May Jul Sep Nov	1995 Jan Mar May Jul Sep Nov
FACILITY			
Sign lease	—		
Order furniture	—		
Order equipment	—		
Occupy office	—		
EMPLOYEES			
Hire administrative assistant		—	
Hire graphic designer		—	
Hire production artist			—
Hire marketing administrator			—
MISCELLANEOUS			
Promo/Advertising		—	
Cash injection		—	

3-59

- **Risk Analysis and Alternative Plans of Action**

    Sales Projections – sales forecasts are based on inflated hours per month (30-40). Hours would have to fall below 20 before there would be a cash flow concern. If this did happen, the budget would be recalculated to exclude contract work, advertising, planned purchases and moving expenses.

    Unavailable Capital – planned expansion in 1994 will not be possible. If the Denver Metro area is not able to meet growth and capital needs, relocation to another city or State may be desirable.

- **Salvaging Assets**

Siempre Envisions will initially be a home-based p1art-time business. Consequently, it can at any time cease to do business with little financial repercussions. Current personal assets are a Macintosh personal computer, printer, telephone and office desk which will be kept by Catherine Hawthorne in the event of business closure. Siempre Envisions will make every possible attempt to secure payment for any outstanding invoices.

Growth Plan

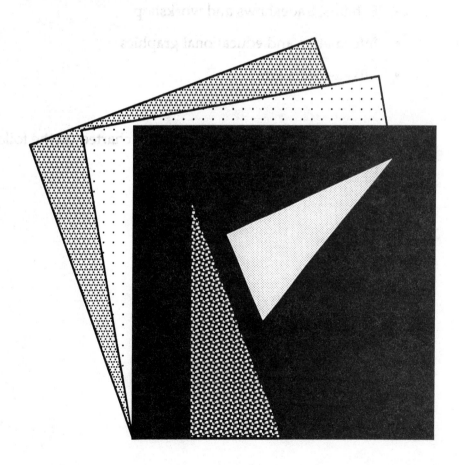

Growth Plan

- **New Offerings to Market**

    Expanding into other art forms and computer technologies by late 1995 may by explored with other companies or individuals. In the visual media area there are several new services that Siempre Envisions could offer:

    - 3-D and video production
    - Exhibits, tradeshows and workshop
    - Information and educational graphics
    - Mixed-media arts

    The most exciting new offerings are charted on the following page.

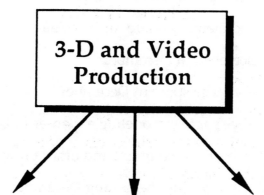

- Retirement community
  - recreation center
  - golf course
  - nature walk

- Education
  - self instruction
  - general information

- International trade
  - travelog
  - product advertising
  - cultural exchange

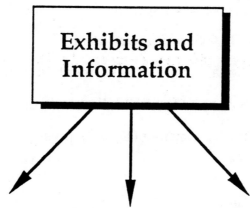

- Tradeshows
  - exhibitor promo
  - exhibit layout

- Museum
  - lobby signage
  - exhibit display
  - maps

- Non-Profit & Service
  - cross-cultural awareness
  - arts and festivals
  - newsletters
  - posters

♦ ♦ ♦

- **Capital Requirements**

  Small business loan - $10,000 for November, 1993

  - Purchase of expanded memory board and modem
  - Company sign silkscreened in December
  - Lease deposit on new office space in December.
  - Moving and new office space remodeling expenses in December.
  - Small business attorney, tax accountant and other professional services
  - Installation of 4 new phone lines beginning December 15
  - Utilities deposit on new office space December 15
  - Corporate ID, resale license, filing, name search
  - Miscellaneous expenses for incorporation
  - General promotion for new business and location.
  - General advertising in yellow pages

  Small business loan - $10,000 for January, 1994

  - Furniture and additional computer equipment, laser printer
  - Summer college intern hired for credit. Pay commission of $600
  - Wages for administrative assistant (12 mo.), president (12 mo.) and production artist (6 mo.)
  - General operating funds
  - Business inventory and office supplies
  - Booth at the Denver Advertising conference in May
  - Yellow pages advertisement
  - 40 shares of common stock issued

◆ **Personnel Requirements**

A **production artist** will be contracted in the June, 1992 to assist in the creation, production, and coordination of promotional marketing materials.

The **administrative assistant** will provide administrative and clerical support to the CEO and Marketing Department. This person will be hired in March, 1994.

The **marketing administrator** will develop marketing strategies, perform market planning and analysis and coordinate outside sales. This person will be on board in February, 1995.

The **graphic designer** position requires excellent board production skills, understanding of 4-color graphics, and advanced Macintosh ability using Quark Xpress and FreeHand software. This position will be filled in September, 1995.

◆ **Exit Strategies**

1) Sell personally-held stock to the other shareholders
2) Go out of business and liquidate assets
3) Find employment with another company
4) Start a new venture and transfer assets to the new company

The ideal exit strategy is either #1 or #4. Currently, negotiations are continuing with an interior designer in New Jersey to pursue a joint venture. Talks are also ongoing with a sales manager at TWA airlines in Los Angeles to pursue a joint international travel venture.

CHAPTER 4
EAST SIDE PLATING COMPANY

Written by:

    Jack P. Osten
    1994 FastTrac Graduate
    Kauffman Foundation, Kansas City, MO

Computer hardware:

    IBM

Computer software:

    Word Perfect 5.1, Lotus 1,2,3

Printing:

    Ink Jet Printer

Book used to write business plan :
    <u>The Entrepreneur's Planning Handbook</u>

Overview

Because of downsizing, Jack was leaving his job at Marion Merrell Dow and attended the Premier FastTrac II training program in Kansas City, MO sponsored by the Kauffman Foundation. While going through outplacement at the Transition Center with Right Associates, Jack met an instructor who mentioned that he had a metal plating business. Jack needed some work done on his chrome car bumpers and asked the instructor if his company would do the work. The instructor explained that his business was going through bankruptcy and would be auctioned in the near future.

Jack became interested in this business and the potential to purchase it. He started researching the metal plating business and wrote his business plan with the idea of bidding on the business. He researched the industry, called over 80 customers of the business, performed other due diligence, and found while writing his business plan that the business could be profitable and would be a good buy.

Jack secured a bank loan with an SBA guarantee for $220,000 to use for buying and operating the business. Four days before auction, he was informed by the banker that his loan was conditionally approved with a slight contingency. Jack would need to obtain a Phase 2 Soil Audit on the property to check for possible illegal dumping of chemicals before monies from the loan could be dispersed. Jack tried everything to obtain the audit before the auction but, found out that it was impossible to obtain the audit that quickly.

His options were not to bid on the business at the auction, or take the risk of buying the business without a loan. If successful at the auction, he would be required to make a $10,000 non-refundable deposit on the property. Therefore, even though the business plan showed that the venture could be quite profitable, he decided not to bid on the business. He is currently looking for another business to purchase.

Although Jack wrote his business plan quickly, it was thorough and complete. Three different banks said they would approve his loan if they obtained an SBA loan guarantee. Because of the timing, Jack did not write his plan using fancy graphics, charts, or other visuals. This is an example of a well-written plan without much graphic design. It is akin to many plans written by FastTrac graduates.

The East Side Plating business plan is easy to read and follow. Jack used all the suggested subtitles and formatted the plan in accordance with the The Entrepreneur's Planning Handbook. Each of the bankers he worked with told Jack his business plan was one of the best they had reviewed. It is an excellent example to follow and proves that with a minimum investment, the business could be profitable and worth purchasing.

BUSINESS PLAN CRITIQUE

Name: East Side Plating Company

I. Overall Appearance and Format

Strength:

The design made good use of placing subtitles in the left margin, thereby creating an effective use of white space. This makes it easy for the reader to focus on the details of the plan as well as quickly being able to find various sections.

The length of plan is appropriate for this business at approximately 45 pages.

Weakness:

It fails to use graphs, charts and pictures to give readers a visual appearance of the company. The easier it is to scan a business plan and look at graphics, the more likely investors will read and review the plan.

II. Cover Page

Weakness:

It fails to include a picture of the products that the manufacturing process enhances.

It does not include a contact person including address and telephone numbers to make it easier for readers to contact the entrepreneur.

III. Table of Contents

Strength:

It is complete and includes page numbers for all sections.

IV. Executive Summary

Strength:

All the major areas listed in the Entrepreneur's Planning Handbook are addressed in the Executive Summary.

BUSINESS PLAN CRITIQUE

Weakness:

It is not in letter form. This business plan was written to secure funding from a bank and should have been addressed to the loan officer(s) involved.

It does not list infrastructure support team; i.e., lawyer, accountant, banker, etc.

It does not mention the major competitors of the company.

It does not discuss how much money is needed to purchase the business out of bankruptcy.

The Executive Summary usually should not be longer than two pages. The entrepreneur could better summarize this information.

V. Management and Organization

Strength:

The job descriptions and why each person is qualified to perform identified responsibilities are well described.

Advisory Council information is complete and gives names, addresses, but it does not include telephone numbers for the council members.

Weakness:

It does not give correct titles for Board of Directors; i.e., Chairman of the Board, Secretary, Treasurer, and Directors.

Management organization chart is located in the Appendix instead of being placed in this section.

This section should indicate, as a footnote, that resumes of the management team are located in the Appendix.

VI. Product/Service

Weakness:

<u>Trademarks, Patents, Copyrights, Licenses, Royalties</u>

There is not a detailed discussion of the proprietary rights.

<u>Product Limitation</u>

The entrepreneur fails to identify if any product limitations exist and how

BUSINESS PLAN CRITIQUE

they will be dealt with.

Spin-offs

More detail should be given to possible new products or services that could be added in the future. This will give the reader confidence that there is good growth potential. Potential new products to replace obsolete products should also be included.

Since the entrepreneur is going to a bank for financing, the lender is interested in finding out how the loan will be paid off in the future with increasing new sales from spin-offs.

Production

This subtitle has been deleted.

Manufacturing Facilities

This subtitle has been deleted. The lender will require a detailed description of the facility and the manufacturing process in order to understand the business.

Environmental Impact

This section should be expanded since the lender will be concerned about treatment of the hazardous waste generated by the plating process.

In the Industry Study of the Marketing section of the plan, the entrepreneur states that companies that are coating products are closing at a high rate because of environmental requirements. But it makes no reference to this statement under this section. How the company handles hazardous waste generated and how this impacts the business needs to be explained.

VII. Marketing Plan

Strength:

Competition

There is a good description of the competitors and the research on the competition is complete.

Market Penetration

This section is to the point and details how the market will be penetrated.

BUSINESS PLAN CRITIQUE

Weakness:

Customer Profile

This subtitle is missing from the plan.

Target Market Profile

This section is missing from the plan. The entrepreneur has a good market penetration strategy. However, failing to mention the customer profile and target market suggests to the reader that the entrepreneur does not know his customer and has not conducted proper research to identify new customers that the company might solicit.

Market Penetration

The entrepreneur does not include who would be contacting the customers and closing the sales.

VIII. Financial Plan

Strength:

There is good research on expenses. Cash Flow documents and the Income statements are well done.

Weakness:

Assumptions

Assumptions do not correspond with the Chart of Accounts in the Cash Flow documents. There are no numbers in the Cash Flow to correspond and cross-reference with numbered assumptions.

IX. Operating System

Weakness:

Planning Chart

This chart is not included. Since this is an existing business, it should include a Planning Chart on how the money will be obtained, when assets will be evaluated, when existing inventory will be taken, when repairs will be done,

BUSINESS PLAN CRITIQUE

etc.

<u>Risk Analysis</u>

Entrepreneur does not complete and address all of the inherent risks. This indicates to the reader that the entrepreneur has not considered what could happen to the business if projections in the plan are not met.

<u>Salvaging Assets</u>

Reference to salvaging assets is not included. Since the plan is written to secure bank financing, the lender will want to know what assets are salvable in case of failure to recoup money for the loan.

X. Growth Plan

Weakness:

The entrepreneur has not addressed the future growth of the business by adding new sources of sales. It is extremely important to lenders to find good potential for growing the business. This strategy should be explained in the plan.

The entrepreneur fails to discuss any possible exit strategies.

XI. Appendix

Strength:

It includes letters from previous customers who intend to do business with the new owner.

Weakness:

It only includes a resume of the CEO and not the rest of the management team. A copy of the stock option plan should be included. A picture of the facility and its layout should be included.

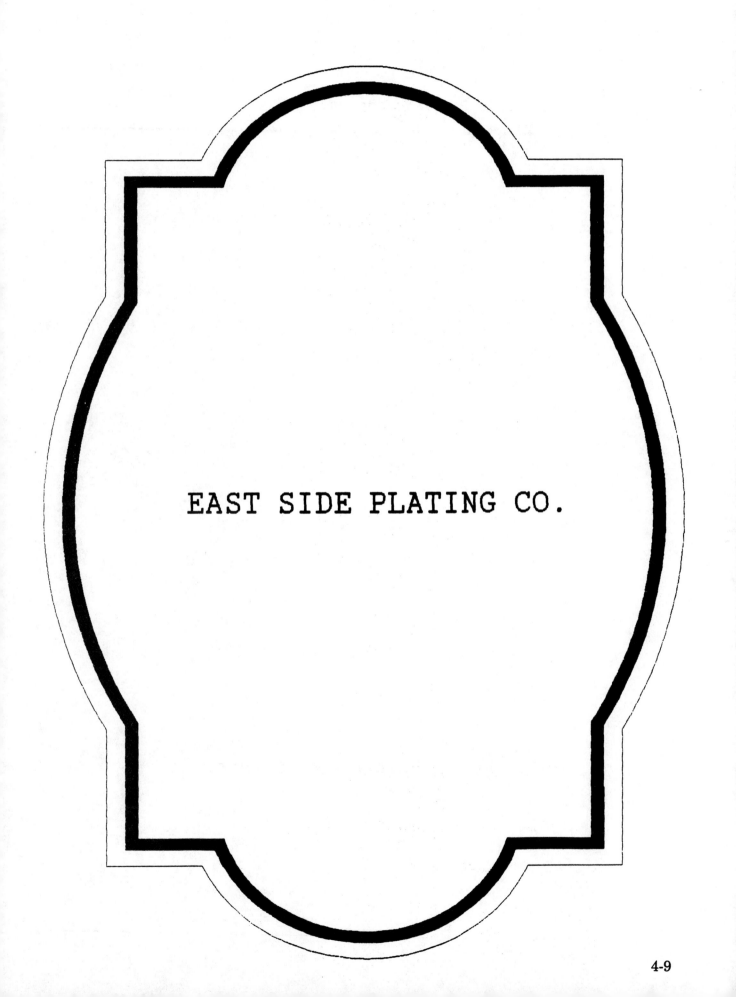

EPC - Eastside Plating Company

Loan request submitted by:

Jack P Osten

and

Marilyn J. Osten

EPC - *Eastside Plating Company*

TABLE OF CONTENTS

EXECUTIVE SUMMARY

MANAGEMENT AND ORGANIZATION

PRODUCT/SERVICE PLAN

MARKETING PLAN

FINANCIAL PLAN

OPERATING SYSTEM

GROWTH PLANS

APPENDIX

EPC - *Eastside Plating Company*

Executive Summary

EPC - *Eastside Plating Company*

Polishing is a process, used before plating, to prepare a metal surface (to smooth) for electroplating. Electroplating of a polished metal places a metal coating on the base metal for protective and decorative reasons. Steel, stainless steel, zinc die-castings, brass and aluminum are base metals that can be plated. These base metals can be plated with zinc, cadmium, copper, nickel and chromium coatings to reduce oxidation (of the base metal).

To "plate" a coating on an object, the object must first be cleaned thoroughly. After cleaning the object is suspended in a water solution containing the metal coating and an electrical current is passed through the object to the solution. This process attracts the plating metal (zinc, cadmium, copper, nickel and/or chromium) from the solution to the object, where it adheres. The amount of current, length of time in the solution and percentage of coating metal in the solution affect the thickness of the coating on the object.

This business will reopen Eastside Plating Company (Company), a metal polishing and electroplating company. The Company has existed for 55 years at 2641 Jackson, Kansas City, MO. During that time the Company had developed an outstanding reputation for quality work (based on over 40 previous customer's comments.)

Eastside Plating Company closed June 17, 1993 due to bankruptcy. As terms of a divorce settlement the previous owners ex-wife wanted a large financial sum from the business. The owner was highly leveraged and could not meet these financial requirements, he filed for corporate (and personal) bankruptcy.

This business offers one unique plating service not found within 200 miles of Kansas City. We have an automatic line that can be used to copper, nickel and chrome plate small to medium sized metal pieces. This line enables us to:

- o Lower our price (less labor)
- o Provide more consistent, uniform plating
- o Copper plate zinc-oxide parts
- o Provide four day turn-around* (for straight plating)

* Previous customers told us they are waiting between two and three weeks.

In addition, we offer other plating services, thus a more complete service, through our barrel line and hand plating (of larger pieces) line. Our barrel line gives us the ability to zinc and cadmium plate small parts (nuts, bolts, etc.) with yellow or clear finishes.

EPC - Eastside Plating Company

We have called 76 of the customers who did business with the Company in 1992. We asked them if they would consider Eastside Plating Company as their vendor of choice should we reopen the doors. With the exception of one customer, they all agreed to consider us. Some told us that Eastside need only open it's doors and they would be back, as evidenced by the letters of intent found in Exhibit A.

The list of over 87 customers includes tool, dental equipment, shelving, furniture and plumbing manufacturers, zinc-diecasters, aeronautical suppliers, and other manufacturers of parts that need to be plated for protective and/or decorative reasons.

Start-up expenditures will be used to purchase chemicals, make minor repairs and install a water treatment system. The water treatment system, designed for the Company and purchased 4 years ago, will enable the Company to meet EPA and local water pollution control standards.

We will be organized as a C corporation for easy disbursement of funds, liability protection and for tax benefits. The Company will be run by Jack Osten a graduate of business, University of Wisconsin, Milwaukee.

Jack Osten, President, will be responsible for the daily production and sales calls to new and existing customers. Marilyn Osten will be Executive Vice President and will administer the financial controls of the Company.

We have three major competitors in the plating business in the Kansas City area; Missouri Plating Company, Kansas City Plating Works, De Tray Plating Works Company and other minor competitors. An analysis of these platers capabilities is included in the Marketing Plan, see Page 17.

We will be a strong competitor using a personalized letter campaign to previous customers as well as potential new customers. A profile listing of over 1,200 companies, whose services and/or products lend themselves to electroplating, has been obtained for the potential customer mailing. A brochure will be included with the letter to the previous and potential customers.

Our terms will be net 30 days to customers with established credit. We are also considering adding a new pricing strategy. We may offer 1% discounts for every $5,000 in orders for the year, up to a maximum of 4%. This may encourage the customers to send us all of their plating orders. It will also give our smaller customers, who would not otherwise get any discount, a price break.

EPC - Eastside Plating Company

MANAGEMENT AND OPERATIONS TEAM

An Organization Chart is included as Exhibit B.

Jack P. Osten, C.E.O.

Jack graduated from the University of Wisconsin Milwaukee with a BS in Production Management. He has been working in the business environment for 32 years and brings knowledge and commitment to this venture. He will devote all his time and $71,500 to get this business reopened. His experience as an auditor and consultant for Price Waterhouse & Co., Carlson Companies, Inc. and Marion Merrill Dow Inc. gives him knowledge and experience with control systems, accounting systems, managing and dealing with people, and meeting deadlines. Also, he was a United Way Campaign Loaned Executive in 1985 and President of the Church Council which gave him additional experience in the afore mentioned areas. Jack's resume is included as Exhibit C.

C.E.O. RESPONSIBILITIES

- Maintaining adequate funding.
- Initiating and maintaining advertising and marketing efforts.
- Oversee all of the business operations, e.g. production, financial, etc..
- Day-to-day Operations controls.
- Oversee financial planning and control.
- Hiring and terminations of employees with the recommendation of the Plant Manager.

Marilyn J. Osten, Executive Vice President

Marilyn has worked 30 years in the business environment for manufacturing firms such as Maico Hearing Instruments and General Electric. Marilyn brings personal computer knowledge and experience as well as organizational skills to this venture.

EXECUTIVE VICE PRESIDENT RESPONSIBILITIES

- Payroll preparation (checks, IRS statements).
- Posting of Accounts Receivable checks.
- Customer correspondence.

EPC - *Eastside Plating Company*

Lewis Miller, Plant Manager

Lewis had worked for Eastside Plating Co. for 28 years. He started in the plant as a polisher, was lead polisher, Assistant Plant Manager and was promoted to Plant Manager two years ago. Lewis has excellent customer recognition and rapport with the customers. In fact, many asked if Lewis would be working for us.

PLANT MANAGER RESPONSIBILITIES

- Assist the shop floor personnel in the performance of their responsibilities.
- Daily scheduling of the automatic plating line, hand plating line and polishing shop.
- Daily attendance reporting.
- Daily production reporting.
- Oversee the quality of the polishing and plating operations.
- Release of customer orders for pickup.
- Oversee the training of new personnel.
- Performance reviews of plating and maintenance personnel.
- Making sure all performance reviews are completed in a timely manner.
- Setting prices on new customer orders.
- Make sure that all chemical tanks are at peak plating/cleaning capabilities.
- Keeping equipment in proper working order.
- Training the Assistant Plant Manager.

James Pemberton, Assistant Plant Manager

James worked for the Company for one year. He was promoted to plater one month after starting to work for the Company and ran the second shift plating operation. His promotion to Assistant Plant Manager is recommended by Jim Hurt (the previous owner), Lewis Miller (Plant Manager) and Ray Evert (outside consultant).

ASSISTANT *PLANT MANAGER RESPONSIBILITIES*

- Perform all Plant Manager responsibilites as assigned by the Plant Manager.
- Be responsible for all Plant Manager activities in the absence of the Plant Manager.
- Initially Jim will be our maintenance man.

EPC - Eastside Plating Company

Wayne Cornett, Lead Polisher

Wayne worked for 10 years at Eastside Plating Company. He started out as a polisher and was one of the lead polishers when the plant closed.

LEAD POLISHER RESPONSIBILITES

o Train new polishers.
o Assist the Plant Manager in daily scheduling of the Polish Shop.
o Performance reviews of Polish Shop personnel.
o Assist the Polish Shop personnel in the performance of their responsibilities.
o Oversee the quality of the polishing operations.

Dottie Feller, Administrative Assistant

Having worked for this Company for 23 years, Dottie brings a great deal of knowledge and understanding to this responsibility. Like Lewis Miller, she has great customer recognition and rapport.

ADMINISTRATIVE ASSISTANT RESPONSIBILITIES

o Telephone contact with customers. (Customer Service).
o Customer billing.
o Payroll record keeping.
o Scheduling of the Barrel Line (co-ordinating customer orders with the Plant Manager).
o Posting of general ledger transactions.
o Daily calculation of production performance.
o Purchase of chemicals per the Plant Manager.
o Preparation of accounts payable.

John Spencer, Plater

John worked for Eastside Plating for over 10 years.

PLATER RESPONSIBILITIES

o Copper, nickle and chrome plate customer orders per the schedule on the automatic or hand plating lines.

EPC - *Eastside Plating Company*

James Spencer, Barrel line operator	James operated the Eastside Plating barrel line for over 12 years.

<u>*BARREL LINE OPERATOR RESPONSIBILITIES*</u>

o Cadmium and zinc plate customer ordered parts per the schedule.

Anyone who works for Eastside Plating Company will be an associate, we will not use the term employee. The reason for this is that we all work together, for the good of the company, and will all share in the profits.

EPC - *Eastside Plating Company*

Management
and Organization

EPC - Eastside Plating Company

Company Ownership	*Members*	*Position*	*Ownership*
	Jack Osten	CEO	50%
	Marilyn Osten	Executive Vice President	50%

A "C" corporation will be formed when we acquire Eastside Plating Company in November 1993.

The number of authorized shares is anticipated at 15,000.

Compensation

Jack Osten will be paid an annual salary of $65,600 beginning February 1993, he is drawing a salary through Jauary 1994 from Marion Merrell Dow Inc. Marilyn Osten will take out a salary after sales exceed the expenses (after break-even).

Board of Directors

Name	*Title*
Jack Osten	CEO
Marilyn Osten	Executive Vice President
Kelly Osten	Director at Large

EPC - Eastside Plating Company

Advisory Council	We have just begun to form our Advisory Council. At this time we are planning on asking the following individuals to participate in this activity.

Lee Baty
Attorney
Field, Gentry & Benjamin
600 E. 11
Kansas City, MO 64106

* 50 % of Mr. Baty's clients are small businesses.

Rodger Marsh
Accountant
Marsh W. Rodger & Associates
800 W 47th St.
Suite 410
Kansas City, MO 64112

* All of Mr. Marsh's clients are small businesses.

Ray Evert
Outside Consultant
5033 NE 57 Terr.
Kansas City, MO 641119

* Ray Evert worked for Eastside Plating for 31 years before retiring. At the time of his retirement he was the Plating Manager.

Lewis Miller
Plant Manager
East Side Plating Company

* Eastside associate.

Craig Roeder
Mark Twain Bank South
10401 Holmes
Kansas City, Missouri

* Loan officer at lending institution.

EPC - *Eastside Plating Company*

Insurance

Eastside Plating will have a $250,000 insurance policy on Jack Osten. The policy will be issued through:

>Oliver & Shopen Insurance Agency
>6920 W 79th Street
>P.O. Box 2199
>Shawnee Mission, Kansas 66201
>*(Attn: Bill Adams)*

Profit Sharing

We will establish a Profit Sharing Plan (Plan) for all associates based on position and individual performance. All full time associates are eligible to participate beginning their first year. Initially the Company will contribute 10% of gross sales that exceed operating expenses (minus depreciation) at the end of the year.

Following is a list of positions and the number of Profit Sharing shares the position is granted:

Position	*Shares*
Plant Manager	3
Assistant Plant Manager	2
Lead Polisher	2
Administrative Assistant	2
All other positions	1

Performance and related factor to be applied to Shares:

Performance	*Factor*
o Poor performance	0 (zero)%
o Average performance	50%
o Above average performance	100%

Profit Sharing Calculation:

An individual's performance factor is multiplied times their shares to determine the total number of shares they will receive. The number of shares (for all associates) is totaled and divided into the total dollars to be distributed. This value per share is multiplied times the individuals number of shares to determine the amount each asssociate will receive.

EPC - Eastside Plating Company

Product/Service Plan

EPC - Eastside Plating Company

PRODUCT

Purpose

Products are electroplated for protective and decorative purposes. There is a market for quality plating on a timely basis at a reasonable and competitive price.

Features

Our automated line provides us with cost and quality advantages over our competitors. The cost advantage is realized through fewer direct labor hours. Two employees load the line; 45 minutes later two employees unload the line and perform a quality inspection at the same time.

Our quality, on the automated line, is achieved by applying a consistent thickness of plating to each customers part. In a manual process (where items to be plated are moved manually to the various plating tanks) any extra time in one of the tanks will increase the thickness of the plating. Through the automated line we can use electrical current to plate each piece with the thickness of coating that is consistent with customer requirements.

History

This business has been operating for 55 years in the same location. At the moment it is closed due to bankruptcy. The bankruptcy was not due to a business related problem but a personal financial problem of the owner.

Research and Development

We will research the installation of an Air Filtration System in the next few years. This is necessary to reduce the health risk to employees, reduce the humidity in the building (which greatly affects the equipment) and to meet anticipated EPA clean air standards.

Patents and Trade Secrets

Our customer list is a Trade Secret.

EPC - Eastside Plating Company

Government Regulations and Approvals	We will need to follow OSHA, EPA and Kansas City Water and Pollution Control regulations for the use, storage, discharge and disposal of water and chemicals. The water treatment system that will be installed, before we open our doors to business, will greatly reduce the risk of our accidentally violating any regulations during the discharge of water.

We will need to get a permit from the Kansas City Water and Pollution Control Department, the EPA for the removal of hazardous waste, a Merchant's permit, and a sales tax permit before we open for business, January 1, 1994. |
| Liabilities | Our use of chemicals requires that we train our associates in the proper use, storage and discharge of these chemicals as determined by OSHA. We will provide this training yearly. A record will be kept, with the employee's signature, indicating the date they received the training.

As was mentioned earlier, we will be investigating the installation of an air purification system. One of the most important reasons is to reduce any potential health risk to our associates. |
Related Services	We will offer polishing to enhance the appearance and quality of the product. Our expectation is that this will be 30 - 40 percent of our sales.
Spin-Offs	We will consider black oxide plating in 1995. At that time we will need to look at the market for this plating and whether we can provide this service at a profit.
Environmental Impact	The water purification system will purify the water before it is discharged. We will recycle all chemicals that can be reused. Recycled paper will be purchased for office use.

EPC - **Eastside Plating Company**

Marketing Plan

EPC - Eastside Plating Company

INDUSTRY PROFILE AND COMPETITION

Industry Overview and Size

In number of plating and polishing shops decreased during the years 1982 to 1989:
- 1982....3,450
- 1988....3,203

United States, Manufacturing USA, 3rd Edition - Exhibit D. Enforcement of tougher water and air pollution controls will make it more difficult for smaller shops to stay in business.

Growth Potential

The plating industry production grew slightly:
- 1982 ....$ 2,731.4 (millions)
- 1989 ....$ 4,513.3 (millions)

Exhibit D.

Over 20 of the previous customers of the Company have informed us of their dissatisfaction with their current vendors. The most common complaint was that they were getting poor quality plating. The second most common complaint was that they were waiting 2 - 3 weeks to get their products plated.

The declining number of platers, increase in orders, and complaints from previous customers indicate that there is a market for a plater who can provide quality work in a short time frame. We will be positioned to provide our customers with quality plating in 4 days (plating only, no polishing).

Industry Trends

The trend in the plating industry, as with all industry, is to automate to reduce the labor overhead. This is evidenced by the increase in capital investment:
- 1982 .... $78,000,000
- 1990 ....$119,000,000

(Exhibit D). Our automatic line gives us an advantage over most of our competitors in Kansas City who do not have automatic lines (Reference Exhibit E).

EPC - *Eastside Plating Company*

Profit Characteristics	An hourly labor rate is used to determine the cost/profit for the polishing and manual plating processes. The profit contribution for barrel line plating is based on the number of pounds of material to be plated. The profit for the automatic line is based on "rack" price. We have a minimum order charge of $45 to cover small orders where the value of the work to be completed would be less than $45, using the pricing formulas.
Distribution Network	We will contact the 87+ previous customers and a list of 1,256 companies, whose industry profiles match the products/services of Eastside's previous customers, to begin our operation.
Basis of Competition	Competition in the industry is based on the following factors, in descending order: Quality, turn-around time and price. One interesting point that was mentioned to us by three of the previous customers, the reason they used Eastside before was because Eastside was personable.
Competition Summary	There are 20 other plating companies in the greater Kansas City area. A Competitive Analysis Chart is included as Exhibit E.
	Our biggest competitor, Missouri Plating Company, has an automatic line. However, they do not have a copper plating tank on this line. In order to nickle plate zinc die-castings they must copper plate the pieces off the line and then run these pieces through their automatic line. In addition, Missouri Plating Company does not do any polishing.
	None of the other platers in town have automatic lines for their nickle, chrome plating processes. This means they must manually move the pieces being plated to the various tanks during the plating process. To make a comparison, our automatic line will put a part through 22 separate tanks before the part comes off the line.

EPC - *Eastside Plating Company*

Competition Summary (cont'd)

Eastside plating has several advantages over our competitors; previous customers have commented on the quality, we have an automatic line through which we can offer fast turn-around and we have great rapport with our customers.

We do not expect any problems re-entering the market. This is evidenced by the remark that Missouri Plating Company made to a chemical salesman. They would be happy to have us back in the market to relieve the pressure of all the phone calls they are getting and the pressure they are getting to turn the work around.

Market Penetration

We will contact the previous customers when we reopen Eastside Plating. During our initial conversation with 76 customers all of them said they would definitely give us a chance to bid on future orders. All but one customer made favorable comments about the quality and how pleased they were with Eastside's previous work. Based on these comments and our committments to quality and fast turn-around we are convinced that we can get the greater majority of them back.

Four of the previous customers indicated that they would definitely return to Eastside should we reopen the doors (see Exhibit A). Based on last years sales (and 1993 sales - Ernies Carts), this represents $195,000 + in sales:

	1992 Sales
Carpenter Industries, Inc.	$ 72,115
Granco Industries Corp.	33,504
Lyons Diecasting Company	82,302
	187,921
Ernies Shopping Cart Spec.	7,200 (1993 sls)
Total Sales	$ 195,121 +

We will be able to offer our customers quality plating with a four day turn-around. Plating is one of the last processes to be completed before the product is shipped to our customer's client. Quite frequently there have been delays, in the processes, before the plater gets the parts for plating. Many plating customers expect the plater to make up for this lost time. Our ability to do straight plating in four days will help our customers gain part of their lost time.

EPC - *Eastside Plating Company*

Market Penetration (cont'd)	We also have a profile list of 1,256 companies whose products and/or services are similar to to Eastside's previous customers. Letters, with enclosed brochures, will be sent to all of these potential customers. We will follow-up with a phone call to answer any questions and provide any other information.

We will initially concentrate our market search in Iowa, Kansas, Missouri and Arkansas. In 1995 we will survey our current and previous customers in states such as North Carolina and Ohio. The survey will tell us which factors influenced them to do business with us and could lead to market penetration outside the four state area. |
| Advertising | We will survey our customers in late 1994. One of the questions will be whether they used trade magazines to obtain services, if so which trade magazines. The results of this part of the survey will be used to determine whether we will advertise in trade magazines. We will also subscribe to local trade magazines to see if other local platers advertise in the magazines. |
| Trade Shows | The 1994 survey will also include a question about whether our customers attend trade shows and if they use these shows to obtain services. Based on their responses we will consider exhibiting in some of the trade shows:

o Industrial Expo 'XX (XX equals current year), held in Joplin in September.
o Wichita Industrial Trade Show and Technical Conference, held in February.
o The North American Diecasters Association, regional trade show (date and time tbd).
o Industrial Show, Kansas City, MO in May.

We will attend these trade shows to determine if there are any other platers with displays and the kinds of activities the displays generate. |

EPC - *Eastside Plating Company*

Other Markets

There are a number of car clubs in Kansas City, e.g. The Cadillac Club, Mustangs on Display, etc. We will be sending the presidents of these clubs a letter and promotion in December 1993 to tell them that we are opening for business and would like to meet their member's plating requirements.

We will also be contacting companies that do their own plating, e.g Hallmark, Square D, in 1994 to offer to do their overflow work.

Guarantees

We will guarantee our customers quality plating and polishing. If we do not plate or polish the customer's product properly, we will correct the problem at no additional charge to the customer. Sometimes there are things in the customer's processes that negatively impact polishing and plating. Where we have problems plating a customer's parts, due to a problem with the part, we will work with the customer to correct the situation.

Pricing Profile

In plating and polishing, pricing is done by the "piece". The price is determined per the methods that follow. Where pieces are similar to some we have already priced, we will use the established price.

The cost (per piece) for polishing is determined by the number we can polish in one hour divided into the cost of $30.

For hand plating the number of pieces that can be plated in an hour is divided into $50 to determine the price per piece.

On the barrel line we charge $.11 per pound for plating.

We will charge $15 per rack on our automated line. A rack will hold from one-to-many individual pieces. The rack price of $15 will be divided by the number of pieces that will fit on the rack to determine the customer's price per piece.

4-33

EPC - *Eastside Plating Company*

Pricing Profile (cont'd)

We will offer our customers quantity discounts.

We are also considering a new pricing strategy. One percent discounts will be offered for every $5,000 in orders for the year, e.g. after $5,000 in sales, the customer will receive a one percent discount at $10,000 another one percent discount, at $15,000 another, to a maximum of $20,000. From $20,000 (and up) they would receive a four percent discount.

This discount policy is unique to the plating industry in the Kansas City area. At least two previous customers used other platers at the same time they were using Eastside. With a discount there is an incentive for our customers to send us all of their plating/polishing requirements.

Another reason for a discount policy is that we want to be able to give our smaller customers a price break. We found that many of our smaller customers were in close contact with one another. Word of mouth advertising, about our discounts, may lead to additional customers.

EPC - Eastside Plating Company

Financial Plan

EPC - *Eastside Plating Company*

Assumptions for Financials	For the years 1993-94 through 1998.

Year One (Dec 1993-1994)

We are requesting a loan of $220,00 from Mark Twain Bank South. $89,000 of this amount will be used for working capital, $131,000 will be used to purchase the business (through auction).

Our Fiscal year will be the same as the calendar year. We are anticipating opening on or around January 3, 1994. In light of this, we have combined the December 1993 and 1994 financial statements.

Following are financial assumptions that were made in the development of the Cash Flow Analyses, Income Statements and Balance Sheets included in this section.

1. *Beginning Cash Balance*, Cash Flow Analysis. This is the amount of cash from the previous month's operation (or previous year's balance in years 1995 - 98).

2. *Mark Twain Bank South*, Cash Flow Analysis. The amount borrowed from Mark Twain Bank South.

3. *Sale of Capital Stock*, Cash Flow Analysis. This is the amount we will invest in the business.

4. *Sales (Plating Sales)*, Cash Flow Analysis and Income Statement. Projected sales by month (year 1994) by year (years 1995 - 98). The actual sales for the business, during the years 1989 through 1992, were used to develop these figures.

5. *Accounts Receivable*, Cash Flow Analysis and Balance Sheet. The amount shown in the December 1993 Accounts Receivable ($2,500) is the cash deposit to the Water Department. See *Water* (number 25 below) for a more detailed explanation. It was calculated that 90 percent of the monthly sales would be credit sales (*Accounts Receivable*) and 10 percent would be cash sales.

EPC - Eastside Plating Company

6. *Cash Sales*, Cash Flow Analysis. These are the cash sales for the month (Sales - Accounts Receivable).

7. *Collect Receivables*, Cash Flow Analysis. These are the receivables (from the previous month) that have been collected.

8. *Cash Received - Year*, Cash Flow Analysis. This is the sum of *Beginnning Cash Balance*, *Cash Sales* and *Collect Receivables*.

9. *Interest Income (Interest/Invest Inc.)*, Cash Flow Analysis and Income Statement. This was estimated based on the sales.

10. *Total Cash Available*, Cash Flow Analysis. This is the sum of *Cash Received - Year* and *Interest Income*.

11. *Plating Supplies*, Cash Flow Analysis and Income Statements. We need $17,000 worth of chemicals to bring the plating tanks up to proper plating requirements. This amount is based on chemical analyses that were performed by Goad Chemical Company just before Eastside closed.

12. *Labor*, Cash Flow Analysis and Income Statements. We will need to add two more people, a maintenance person and polisher, in March and April of 1994 to be able to meet our schedules. Also, the December 1993 amounts are for 3 weeks worth of work to get the plant ready to open on January 2, 1994. We will not have a work force between December 24, 1993 and January 3, 1994.

Jack Osten will not draw a salary until February 1994. He is receiving a salary through January 1994 through Marion Merrell Dow as part of the Reduced In Force package.

EPC - *Eastside Plating Company*

13. *Advertising*, Cash Flow Analysis and Income Statements. Our only *Advertising* at first will be the direct mail campaign to the former customers. The amount reflected in December 1993 includes type-setting the brochure, printing 3,000 copies of the broshure and postage to send out the letters and brochures.

14. *Freight*, Cash Flow Analysis and Income Statements. This is the cost to ship some of our customer's work back to them.

15. *Interest (Loans)*, Cash Flow Analysis and Income Statements. This is the interest paid on the loans.

16. *Principal Repayment*, Cash Flow Analysis. This is the amount of loan principal being repaid.

17. *Electricity*, Cash Flow Analysis and Income Statements. During the cold weather we will need to use more utiliies.

The monthly amount also includes the $8.00/month bond payment. The Bond was purchased in lieu of making a $2,500 dollar deposit.

18. *Office Supplies*, Cash Flow Analysis and Income Statements. We will purchase the following office supplies:

- o 3,000 sheets of letterhead.....$61.00
- o 3,000 sheets (plain paper)..... 60.00
- o 3,000 envelopes (w/name)....... 88.00
- o 3,000 numbered Accts Receivable (continuous forms).............310.00
- o Computer paper................. 50.00
- o Office supplies, e.g. paper clips, rubber bands, pencils, etc.   282.00
- $ 884.00

19. *Repairs*, Cash Flow Analysis amd income Statements. These are the costs associated with repairing the equipment, e.g. motors, broken automatic line arms, etc.

EPC - Eastside Plating Company

20. *Laundry*, <u>Cash Flow Analysis</u> and <u>Income Statements</u>. The cost of work rags and other cleaning shop supplies.

21. *Telephone*, <u>Cash Flow Analysis</u> and <u>Income Statements</u>. We will pay the $339 in back charges from the previous owner, who went through bankruptcy, to acquire the old telephone number. The old number has an advertisment in the Yellow Pages and is known by all of the previous customers.

The breakdown of the charges for the month of December 1993 is as follows:

- Back charges.....................339.00
- Install 2 lines..................115.50
- Install 1 line (computer connection between home and office)........ 57.40
- Monthly charge, 2 lines.........106.16
- Monthly charge, 1 line.......... 44.48
- Long distance................... 37.46

$700.00

22. *Insurance*, <u>Cash Flow Analysis</u> and <u>Income Statements</u>. For a breakdown of insurance costs see Exhibit F. The month of December does not include the health and dental coverage as we will not have hired the employees back, full time. The insurance will be paid quarterly.

23. *Automotive*, <u>Cash Flow Analysis</u> and <u>Income Statements</u>. The initial cost in automotive is to have the car checked out and perform some maintenance.

24. *Acctg & Legal*, <u>Cash Flow Analysis</u> and <u>Income Statement</u>. The initial amount includes the following:

- Attorney's fees to date.........$1,000
- Attorney's fees to incorporate..   750
- Accountant's fees to close year. 1,550

$3,300

25. *Water*, <u>Cash Flow Analysis</u> and <u>Income Statements</u>. The intial month (December 1993) includes a $2,500 deposit to the Water Department. This amount will be returned when the Bond has been purchased. The $2,500 is included in the Accounts Receivable amount for December 1993.

EPC - *Eastside Plating Company*

26. *Shop Supplies*, Cash Flow Analysis amd Income Statements. Gloves, safety glasses, etc.

27. *Outside Services*, Cash Flow Analysis and Income Statements. We will use Ray Evert as a consultant to help us in the start up of Eastside Plating Company.

28. *Outside Testing*, Cash Flow Analysis and Income Statements. Twice a year Eastside Plating Company must take samples of it's discharge (down the city sewers), send the samples out for testing, prepare a report indicating the results of the testing and send the report to the city Water and Pollution Control Department. Eastside must pay the cost of the testing.

29. *Gas*, Cash Flow Analysis and Income Statements. The cost to heat the water used to heat the tanks.

30. *Miscellaneous*, Cash Flow Analysis and Income Statements. The following costs are included in the December total:

- Fix hole in roof.................. 1,800
- Install sewer access (Water and Pollution Control)........................... 2,500
- New door in basement of office..... 500
- New overhead door in plant......... 2,500
- Replace arms on automatic line...... 800
- Weld the copper tank on automatic line............................... 300
- Build station for quality check, autmatic line...................... 400
- Other expenditures as needed....... 3,100

31. *Payroll Taxes*, Cash Flow Analysis and Income Statements. These are the payroll taxes that are paid quarterly.

32. *Licenses and Taxes*, Cash Flow Analysis and Income Statements. Licenses and taxes, other than Payroll and Sales Taxes.

33. *Bad Debts Expense*, Cash Slow Analysis and Income Statements. Allowance for uncollectable Receivables.

EPC - Eastside Plating Company

34. *Sales Tax*, Cash Flow Analysis and Income Statements. The sales tax collected on sales to individuals that request personal plating. This amount is owed to the state of Missouri.

35. *PURCHASE BUSINESS, ASSETS, INSTALL*, Cash Flow Analysis. This is the total for purchasing the business, the office equipment and installing the Water Treatment System. For a breakdown of the the expenditures in this section see Exhibit G.

36. *Depreciation*, Income Statements and Balance Sheets. Depreciation has been calculated at the rates approved by the IRS. Exhibit H shows the breakdown of the depreciation.

Years two through five (1995 - 1998)

37. *Labor*, Cash Flow Analysis and Income Statements. The dollar values in this category include the payment of bonuses, to the employees, based on the previous years achievement (sales exceeded expenditures).

DEPRECIATION & AMORTIZATION SCHEDULE	BEG DATE	BEG VALUE	YEAR 1	YEAR 2	YEAR 3	YEAR 4	YEAR 5	YEAR 6	YEAR 7	YEAR 8	CUM DEP/AMO
VEHICLES:											
Automobile	12/01/93	12000.00	2400.00	3840.96	2304.00	1382.40	1382.40	691.20			12000.00
Truck	12/01/93	6550.00	1310.00	2096.00	1257.60	754.56	754.56	377.28			6550.00
Tot Vehicle		18550.00	3710.00	5936.00	3561.60	2136.96	2136.96	1068.48			18550.00
OFFICE & PLANT EQUIPMENT:											
Typewriter	12/01/93	200.00	28.58	48.98	34.98	24.98	17.86	17.86	17.86	8.92	200.00
Telephones	12/01/93	756.00	108.03	185.14	132.22	94.42	67.51	67.44	67.51	33.72	756.00
Computer	12/01/93	1000.00	142.90	244.90	174.90	124.90	89.30	89.20	89.30	44.60	1000.00
Computer Printer	12/01/93	400.00	57.16	97.96	69.96	49.96	35.72	35.68	35.72	17.84	400.00
Computer Software	12/01/93	800.00	114.32	195.92	139.92	99.92	71.44	71.36	71.44	35.68	800.00
FAX Machine	12/01/93	50.00	7.15	12.25	8.74	6.25	4.47	4.46	4.47	2.23	50.00
Copier	12/01/93	400.00	57.16	97.96	69.96	49.96	35.72	35.68	35.72	17.84	400.00
Answering Machine	12/01/93	50.00	7.15	12.25	8.74	6.25	4.47	4.46	4.47	2.23	50.00
Adding Machines (2)	12/01/93	100.00	14.29	24.49	17.49	12.49	8.93	8.92	8.93	4.46	100.00
Copper Tank Liner	12/01/93	3761.00	537.45	921.07	657.80	469.75	335.86	335.48	335.86	167.74	3761.00
Office Safe	12/01/93	1500.00	214.35	367.35	262.35	187.35	133.95	133.80	133.95	66.90	1500.00
Tools for Plant	12/01/93	500.00	71.45	122.45	87.45	62.45	44.65	44.60	44.65	22.30	500.00
Install Water Treat Sys	12/01/93	21100.00	3015.19	5167.39	3690.39	2635.39	1884.23	1882.12	1884.23	941.06	21100.00
Orig. Off & Plant Equip	12/01/93	77490.00	11073.32	18977.30	13553.00	9678.50	6919.86	6912.11	6919.86	3456.05	77490.00
Tot Equipment		108107.00	15448.49	26475.40	18907.91	13502.56	9653.96	9643.14	9653.96	4821.57	108107.00
PLANT:	12/01/93	26200.00	794.87	794.87	794.87	794.87	794.87	794.87	794.87	794.87	6358.96
TOTAL YEARS DEPRECIATION			19953.36	33206.27	23264.38	16434.39	12585.79	11506.49	10448.83	5616.44	133015.96
MONTHLY DEPRECIATION			1662.78	2767.19	1938.70	1369.53	1048.82	958.87	870.74	468.04	11084.66
LAND	12/01/93	20960.00									
TOTAL EQUIP., PLANT, LAND	12/01/93	161817.00									
YEARLY AMORTIZATION	12/01/93	2018.00	403.60	403.60	403.60	403.60	403.60				2018.00
MONTHLY AMORTIZATION			33.63	33.63	33.63	33.63	33.63				168.17

CASH FLOW ANALYSIS	DEC 93	JAN 94	FEB 94	MAR 94	APR 94	MAY 94	JUN 94	JUL 94	AUG 94	SEP 94	OCT 94	NOV 94	DEC 94	TOTALS 94	TOT 93 & 94
BEGINNING CASH BALANCE:	0.00	86833.21	62030.12	45201.18	21617.94	14845.11	14355.68	6171.56	13513.64	24073.13	25984.95	42274.95	61830.61	418732.08	418732.08
CASH PROVIDED FROM:															
Mark Twain Bank South	220000.00														
Sale of Capital Stock	71000.00														
CASH ADDED	0.00													0.00	0.00
SALES		10000.00	16500.00	23000.00	30000.00	36000.00	40000.00	44000.00	48000.00	52000.00	55000.00	58000.00	55000.00	467500.00	467500.00
Accounts Receivable	2500.00	8800.00	15100.00	21350.00	28250.00	34100.00	37900.00	41750.00	45500.00	49400.00	52300.00	55100.00	52000.00	441550.00	444050.00
Cash Sales	0.00	1200.00	1400.00	1650.00	1750.00	1900.00	2100.00	2250.00	2500.00	2600.00	2700.00	2900.00	3000.00	25950.00	25950.00
Collect Receivables		2500.00	8800.00	15100.00	21350.00	28250.00	34100.00	37900.00	41750.00	45500.00	49400.00	52300.00	55100.00	392050.00	392050.00
CASH RECEIVED - MONTH	291000.00	90533.21	72230.12	61951.18	44717.94	44995.11	50555.68	46321.56	57763.64	72173.13	78084.95	97474.95	119930.61	836732.08	1127732.08
INTEREST INCOME	230.00	226.33	180.58	154.88	111.79	112.49	126.39	115.80	144.41	180.43	195.21	243.69	299.83	2091.83	2321.83
TOTAL CASH AVAILABLE	291230.00	90759.54	72410.70	62106.06	44829.73	45107.60	50682.07	46437.36	57908.05	72353.56	78280.17	97718.63	120230.44	838823.91	1130053.91
Expenses:														0.00	0.00
Plating Supplies	8500.00	9500.00	1000.00	1650.00	2300.00	3000.00	3600.00	4000.00	4400.00	4800.00	5200.00	5500.00	5800.00	50750.00	59250.00
Labor	5000.00	9781.00	16288.00	17371.00	17458.00	17502.00	17502.00	17502.00	17502.00	17502.00	17502.00	17502.00	18377.10	201789.10	206789.10
Advertising	149.00	0	0	0	0	0	0	0	0	0	0	0	500	500.00	649.00
Freight	0.00	80.00	132.00	184.00	240.00	288.00	320.00	352.00	384.00	416.00	440.00	50.00	50.00	2936.00	2936.00
Interest	0.00	1375.00	1362.50	1349.93	1337.28	1324.54	1311.73	1298.84	1285.87	1272.81	1259.68	1246.46	1233.16	15657.80	15657.80
Principal Repayment	0.00	1999.42	2011.92	2024.49	2037.14	2049.88	2062.69	2075.58	2088.55	2101.61	2114.74	2127.96	2141.26	24835.24	24835.24
Electricity	1500.00	1500.00	1500.00	1100.00	1125.00	1250.00	1300.00	1350.00	1400.00	1450.00	1500.00	1550.00	1575.00	16600.00	18100.00
Office Supplies	884.00	30.00	49.50	69.00	90.00	108.00	120.00	132.00	144.00	156.00	165.00	174.00	165.00	1402.50	2286.50
Repairs	0.00	100.00	165.00	230.00	300.00	360.00	400.00	440.00	480.00	520.00	550.00	580.00	550.00	4675.00	4675.00
Laundry	0.00	70.00	115.50	161.00	210.00	252.00	280.00	308.00	336.00	364.00	385.00	406.00	385.00	3272.50	3272.50
Telephone	700.00	180.00	180.00	180.00	180.00	180.00	180.00	180.00	180.00	180.00	180.00	180.00	180.00	2160.00	2860.00
Insurance	1246.57	0.00	0.00	7141.71	0.00	0.00	7141.71	0.00	0.00	7141.71	0.00	0.00	7141.71	28566.84	29813.41
Automotive	400.00	100.00	100.00	100.00	100.00	100.00	100.00	100.00	100.00	300.00	100.00	100.00	100.00	1200.00	1600.00
Acctg & Legal	3300.00	0.00	0.00	300.00	0.00	0.00	300.00	0.00	0.00	300.00	0.00	0.00	1800.00	2700.00	6000.00
Water	4100.00	1700.00	1700.00	1700.00	1700.00	1700.00	1700.00	1700.00	1700.00	1700.00	1700.00	1700.00	1700.00	20400.00	24500.00
Shop Supplies	300.00	0.00	130.00	214.50	299.00	330.00	468.00	520.00	572.00	624.00	676.00	715.00	754.00	5362.50	5662.50
Outside Services	1000.00													0.00	1000.00
Gas	0.00	2200.00	0.00	0.00	400.00	0.00	0.00	2160.00	0.00	0.00	400.00	0.00	0.00	800.00	800.00
Miscellaneous	2100.00	2200.00	2200.00	1900.00	1700.00	1620.00	1944.00	2160.00	2376.00	2592.00	2808.00	2970.00	3132.00	27602.00	29702.00
Payroll Taxes	11900.00	30.00	49.50	69.00	90.00	108.00	120.00	132.00	144.00	156.00	165.00	174.00	165.00	1402.50	13302.50
Licenses & Taxes	1017.22	0.00	0.00	4416.29	0.00	0.00	4549.18	0.00	4191.48	3431.59	3431.59	3431.59	3431.59	16588.54	17605.76
Bad Debts Expense	300.00	0.00	110.00	181.50	253.00	330.00	396.00	440.00	484.00	528.00	572.00	605.00	638.00	4537.50	4837.50
Sales Tax	0.00	0.00	17.60	30.20	42.70	56.50	68.20	75.80	83.50	91.00	98.80	104.60	110.20	779.10	779.10
	0.00	84.00	98.00	115.50	122.50	133.00	147.00	157.50	175.00	182.00	189.00	203.00	210.00	1816.50	1816.50
TOTAL CASH EXPENSES	42396.79	28729.42	27209.52	49448.12	29984.62	30751.92	44510.51	32923.72	33834.92	46368.61	36605.22	35888.02	49639.02	436333.62	478730.41
PURCHASE BUSINESS, ASSETS, INSTALL	162000.00													0.00	162000.00
NET CASH ON HAND	86833.21	62030.12	45201.18	21617.94	14845.11	14355.68	6171.56	13513.64	24073.13	25984.95	42274.95	61830.61	70591.42	402490.29	489323.50

4-43

4 YEAR CASH FLOW ANALYSIS	1995	1996	1997	1998
BEGINING CASH BALANCE:	31961.23	42052.53	70968.79	107194.10
CASH PROVIDED FROM:				
SALES	555000.00	560000.00	565000.00	570000.00
Accounts Receivable	52000.00	41625.00	42000.00	42375.00
CASH ADDED				
Cash Sales	22200.00	22400.00	22600.00	22800.00
Collect Receivables	465500.00	498500.00	521500.00	538000.00
CASH RECEIVED - YEAR	519661.23	562952.53	615068.79	667994.10
INTEREST INCOME	1500.00	1550.00	1600.00	1650.00
TOTAL CASH AVAILABLE	521161.23	564502.53	616668.79	669644.10
Expenses:				
Plating Supplies	61050.00	61600.00	62150.00	62700.00
Labor	225640.83	239682.61	250818.36	261882.48
Advertising	555	560	565	570
Freight	4440.00	4480.00	4520.00	4560.00
Interest	13729.79	11652.08	9413.08	7000.26
Principal Repayment	26763.25	28840.96	31079.96	33492.78
Electricity	14330.00	15100.00	15900.00	16500.00
Office Supplies	250.00	250.00	300.00	300.00
Repairs	3330.00	3360.00	3390.00	3420.00
Laundry	2775.00	2800.00	2825.00	2850.00
Telephone	4440.00	4480.00	4520.00	4560.00
Insurance	30000.00	31000.00	32050.00	33000.00
Automotive	1500.00	1500.00	1500.00	1500.00
Acctg & Legal	2100.00	2100.00	2100.00	2100.00
Water	17800.00	18000.00	18800.00	19400.00
Shop Supplies	11100.00	7215.00	7280.00	7345.00
Outside Sevices	0.00			
Outside Testing	900.00	900.00	900.00	900.00
Gas	29415.00	29680.00	29945.00	30210.00
Miscellaneous	1300.00	1350.00	1400.00	1450.00
Payroll Taxes	18637.93	19797.78	20717.60	21631.49
Licenses & Taxes	6660.00	6720.00	6780.00	6840.00
Bad Debts Expense	837.90	897.30	938.70	968.40
Sales Tax	1554.00	1568.00	1582.00	1596.00
TOTAL CASH EXPENSES	479108.70	493533.73	509474.70	524776.41
NET CASH ON HAND	42052.53	70968.79	107194.10	144867.68

INCOME STATEMENTS

	DEC 93	JAN 94	FEB 94	MAR 94	APR 94	MAY 94	JUN 94	JUL 94	AUG 94	SEP 94	OCT 94	NOV 94	DEC 94	TOTALS 94	TOT 93 & 94
Sales:															
Plating Sales	0.00	10000.00	16500.00	23000.00	30000.00	36000.00	40000.00	44000.00	48000.00	52000.00	55000.00	58000.00	55000.00	467500.00	467500.00
Interest Income	230.00	139.29	134.20	113.99	99.01	93.71	94.86	100.36	108.66	120.85	136.68	155.95	181.31	1478.87	1708.87
Total Sales:	230.00	10139.29	16634.20	23113.99	30099.01	36093.71	40094.86	44100.36	48108.66	52120.85	55136.68	58155.95	55181.31	468978.87	469208.87
Cost of Sales:															
Plating Supplies	8500.00	9500.00	1000.00	1650.00	2300.00	3000.00	3600.00	4000.00	4400.00	4800.00	5200.00	5500.00	5800.00	50750.00	59250.00
Labor	5000.00	9781.00	16288.00	17371.00	17458.00	17502.00	17502.00	17502.00	17502.00	17502.00	17502.00	17502.00	18377.10	201789.10	206789.10
Total Cost of Sales:	13500.00	19281.00	17288.00	19021.00	19758.00	20502.00	21102.00	21502.00	21902.00	22302.00	22702.00	23002.00	24177.10	252539.10	266039.10
GROSS PROFIT:	-13270.00	-9141.71	-653.80	4092.99	10341.01	15591.71	18992.86	22598.36	26206.66	29818.85	32434.68	35153.95	31004.21	216439.77	203169.77
Expenses:															
Advertising	149	0	0	0	0	0	500	0	0	0	0	0	0	500.00	649.00
Freight	0.00	80.00	132.00	184.00	240.00	288.00	320.00	352.00	384.00	416.00	440.00	50.00	50.00	2936.00	2936.00
Interest	0.00	1375.00	1362.50	1349.93	1337.28	1324.54	1311.73	1298.84	1285.87	1272.81	1259.66	1246.46	1233.16	15657.80	15657.80
Electricity	1500.00	1500.00	1500.00	1100.00	1125.00	1250.00	1300.00	1350.00	1400.00	1450.00	1500.00	1550.00	1575.00	16600.00	18100.00
Office Supplies	884.00	30.00	49.50	69.00	90.00	108.00	120.00	132.00	144.00	156.00	165.00	174.00	165.00	1402.50	2286.50
Repairs	0.00	100.00	165.00	230.00	300.00	360.00	400.00	440.00	480.00	520.00	550.00	580.00	550.00	4675.00	4675.00
Laundry	0.00	70.00	115.50	161.00	210.00	252.00	280.00	308.00	336.00	364.00	385.00	406.00	385.00	3272.50	3272.50
Telephone	700.00	180.00	180.00	180.00	180.00	180.00	180.00	180.00	180.00	180.00	180.00	180.00	180.00	2160.00	2860.00
Insurance	1246.57	0.00	0.00	7141.71	0.00	0.00	7141.71	0.00	0.00	7141.71	0.00	0.00	7141.71	28566.84	29813.41
Automotive	400.00	100.00	100.00	100.00	100.00	100.00	100.00	100.00	100.00	100.00	100.00	100.00	100.00	1200.00	1600.00
Acctg & Legal	3300.00	0.00	0.00	300.00	1700.00	0.00	300.00	0.00	0.00	300.00	0.00	0.00	100.00	2700.00	6000.00
Shop Supplies	4100.00	1700.00	1700.00	1700.00	1700.00	1700.00	1700.00	1700.00	1700.00	1700.00	1700.00	1700.00	1700.00	20400.00	24500.00
Outside Services	300.00	0.00	130.00	214.50	299.00	390.00	458.00	520.00	572.00	624.00	676.00	715.00	754.00	5362.50	5662.50
Outside Testing	1000.00	0.00	0.00	0.00	0.00	0.00	0.00	0.00	0.00	0.00	0.00	0.00	0.00	0.00	1000.00
Gas	2100.00	0.00	0.00	0.00	400.00	0.00	0.00	0.00	0.00	0.00	400.00	0.00	0.00	800.00	2900.00
Miscellaneous	11900.00	2200.00	2200.00	1900.00	1700.00	1620.00	1944.00	2160.00	2376.00	2592.00	2808.00	2970.00	3132.00	27602.00	29702.00
Payroll Taxes	1017.22	30.00	49.50	69.00	90.00	108.00	120.00	132.00	144.00	156.00	165.00	174.00	165.00	1402.50	13302.50
Licenses & Taxes	300.00	1017.22	1693.95	1705.12	1575.53	1526.08	1447.57	1408.68	1402.01	1380.75	1349.23	1082.41	993.95	16586.54	17605.76
Amortization	33.63	0.00	110.00	181.50	253.00	330.00	396.00	440.00	484.00	528.00	572.00	605.00	638.00	4537.50	4837.50
Depreciation	33.63	33.63	33.63	33.63	33.63	33.63	33.63	33.63	33.63	33.63	33.63	33.63	33.63	403.56	437.19
Bad Debts Expense	0.00	1662.78	1662.78	1662.78	1662.78	1662.78	1662.78	1662.78	1662.78	1662.78	1662.78	1662.78	1662.78	19953.36	19953.36
Sales Tax	0.00	0.00	17.60	30.20	42.70	56.50	68.20	75.80	83.50	91.00	98.80	104.60	110.20	779.10	779.10
	70.00	84.00	98.00	115.50	122.50	133.60	147.00	157.50	175.00	182.00	189.00	203.00	210.00	1817.10	1887.10
Total Operating Exp.	29000.42	10162.63	11299.96	18427.87	11461.42	11423.13	19940.62	12451.23	12942.79	20850.72	14234.12	13536.88	22585.43	179316.80	208317.22
NET PROFIT (-LOSS)	-42270.42	-19304.34	-11953.76	-14334.88	-1120.41	4168.58	-947.76	10147.13	13263.87	8968.13	18200.56	21617.07	8418.78	37122.97	-5147.45

4-45

4 YEAR INCOME STATEMENTS	1995	1996	1997	1998
Sales:				
Plating Sales	555000.00	560000.00	565000.00	570000.00
Interest/Invest Inc.	1500.00	1550.00	1600.00	1650.00
Total Sales:	556500.00	561550.00	566600.00	571650.00
Cost of Sales:				
Plating Supplies	61050.00	61600.00	62150.00	62700.00
Labor	225640.83	239682.61	250818.36	261882.48
Total Cost of Sales:	286690.83	301282.61	312968.36	324582.48
GROSS PROFIT:	269809.17	260267.39	253631.64	247067.52
Expenses:				
Advertising	555	560	565	570
Freight	4440.00	4480.00	4520.00	4560.00
Interest	13729.79	11652.08	9413.08	7000.26
Electricity	14330.00	15100.00	15900.00	16500.00
Office Supplies	250.00	250.00	300.00	300.00
Repairs	3330.00	3360.00	3390.00	3420.00
Laundry	2775.00	2800.00	2825.00	2850.00
Telephone	4440.00	4480.00	4520.00	4560.00
Insurance	30000.00	31000.00	32050.00	33000.00
Automotive	1500.00	1500.00	1500.00	1500.00
Acctg & Legal	2100.00	2100.00	2100.00	2100.00
Water	17800.00	18000.00	18800.00	19400.00
Shop Supplies	11100.00	7215.00	7280.00	7345.00
Outside Sevices	0.00			
Outside Testing	900.00	900.00	900.00	900.00
Gas	29415.00	29680.00	29945.00	30210.00
Miscellaneous	1300.00	1350.00	1400.00	1450.00
Payroll Taxes	18637.93	19797.78	20717.60	21631.49
Licenses & Taxes	6660.00	6720.00	6780.00	6840.00
Amortization	403.60	403.60	403.60	307.52
Depreciation	33206.27	23264.38	16434.39	12585.79
Bad Debts Expense	837.90	897.30	938.70	968.40
Sales Tax	1316.00	1400.00	1470.00	1512.00
Total Operating Expense	199026.49	186910.14	182152.37	179510.46
NET PROFIT (-LOSS):	70782.68	73357.25	71479.27	67557.06

DEC 31, 1994 BALANCE SHEET

ASSETS

  Current Assets:

    Mark Twain Bank South (MTBS)   70591.42

    Accounts Receivable   52000.00

    Other Intangible Assets   1518.32

  Total Current Assets   124109.74

  Fixed Assets:

    Equipment & Furniture   108107.00

    Vehicles   18550.00

    Building   26200.00

    Land   20960.00

    Reserve for Depreciation   19953.36

  Total Fixed Assets   153863.64

TOTAL ASSETS   277973.38

LIABILITIES AND CAPITAL

  Current Liabilities:

    Accounts Payable   0.00

  Total Current Liabilities   0.00

  Long Term Liabilities:

    Loan Payable to MTBS   195164.76

  Total Long Term Liabilities   195164.76

  Capital:

    Capital Stock   87956.07

    Retained Earnings   -5147.45

  Total Capital   82808.62

TOTAL LIABILITIES & CAPITAL   277973.38

DEC. 31, 1995 BALANCE SHEET

ASSETS

Current Assets:

Mark Twain Bank South	42052.53	
Accounts Receivable	41625.00	
Other Intangible Assets	1114.72	
Total Current Assets		84792.25

Fixed Assets:

Equipment & Furniture	108107.00	
Vehicles	18550.00	
Building	26200.00	
Land	20960.00	
Reserve for Depreciation	53159.63	
Total Fixed Assets		120657.37

TOTAL ASSETS 205449.62

LIABILITIES AND CAPITAL

Current Liabilities:

Accounts Payable	0.00	
Total Current Liabilities		0.00

Long Term Liabilities:

Loan Payable to MTBS	168401.51	
Total Long Term Liabilities		168401.51

Capital:

Capital Stock	-33734.57	
Retained Earnings	70782.68	
Total Capital		37048.11

TOTAL LIABILITIES & CAPITAL 205449.62

DEC. 31, 1996 BALANCE SHEET

ASSETS

Current Assets:

Mark Twain Bank South	70968.79	
Accounts Receivable	42000.00	
Other Intangible Assets	711.12	
Total Current Assets		113679.91

Fixed Assets:

Equipment & Furniture	108107.00	
Vehicles	18550.00	
Building	26200.00	
Land	20960.00	
Reserve for Depreciation	76424.01	
Total Fixed Assets		97392.99

TOTAL ASSETS   211072.90

LIABILITIES AND CAPITAL

Current Liabilities:

Accounts Payable	0.00	
Total Current Liabilities		0.00

Long Term Liabilities:

Loan Payable to MTBS	139560.55	
Total Long Term Liabilities		139560.55

Capital:

Capital Stock	-1844.90	
Retained Earnings	73357.25	
Total Capital		71512.35

TOTAL LIABILITIES & CAPITAL   211072.90

DEC 31, 1997 BALANCE SHEET

ASSETS

Current Assets:
Mark Twain Bank South (MTBS)	107194.10	
Accounts Receivable	42375.00	
Other Intangible Assets	<u>370.52</u>	
Total Current Assets		149939.62

Fixed Assets:
Equipment & Furniture	108107.00	
Vehicles	18550.00	
Building	26200.00	
Land	20960.00	
Reserve for Depreciation	<u>92858.40</u>	
Total Fixed Assets		<u>80958.60</u>

TOTAL ASSETS   230898.22

LIABILITIES AND CAPITAL

Current Liabilities:
Accounts Payable	<u>0.00</u>	
Total Current Liabilities		0.00

Long Term Liabilities:
Loan Payable to MTBS	<u>108480.59</u>	
Total Long Term Liabilities		108480.59

Capital:
Capital Stock	50938.36	
Retained Earnings	<u>71479.27</u>	
Total Capital		<u>122417.63</u>

TOTAL LIABILITIES & CAPITAL   230898.22

DEC 31, 1998 BALANCE SHEET

ASSETS

Current Assets:
Mark Twain Bank South (MTBS)	144867.68	
Accounts Receivable	44000.00	
Other Intangible Assets	0.00	
Total Current Assets		188867.68

Fixed Assets:
Equipment & Furniture	108107.00	
Vehicles	18550.00	
Building	26200.00	
Land	20960.00	
Reserve for Depreciation	105444.19	
Total Fixed Assets		68372.81

TOTAL ASSETS   257240.49

LIABILITIES AND CAPITAL

Current Liabilities:
Accounts Payable	0.00	
Total Current Liabilities		0.00

Long Term Liabilities:
Loan Payable to MTBS	74987.81	
Total Long Term Liabilities		74987.81

Capital:
Capital Stock	114695.62	
Retained Earnings	67557.06	
Total Capital		182252.68

TOTAL LIABILITIES & CAPITAL   257240.49

EPC - *Eastside Plating Company*

Operating System

EPC - *Eastside Plating Company*

POLICIES

Billing Customer

We will bill the customer, who has established credit, the day following the return shipment of the customers product. Customers, who do not have established credit, must pay when they pick up their product or when we deliver it. The credit terms are net 30 days.

Paying Suppliers

We will pay our suppliers according to their schedule. Initially we may have to pay C.O.D., until we have established creditability.
We are working with our major supplier to see if we can pay 50 percent at delivery and the rest in 30 days.

COLLECTING

Accounts Receivable

Customers with estalished credit will receive 30 days to pay their bills. Regular customers who do not prove to be credit worthy will be required to pay for their order when they pick it up, from our office, or when we deliver it. Irregular customers, walk-ins off the street, will be required to pay the full charge for their order when they drop it off.

Guarantees and Returns

We guarantee the quality of all polishing and plating performed by us. If a customer has a problem with their order we will work with the customer to determine the source of the problem and correct it. If we are at fault, we will correct the problem at no charge to the customer.

EPC - Eastside Plating Company

Control Systems

We will institute the following financial control systems.

All customers will be asked to send their payments to a post office box. Jack Osten or Marilyn Osten will get the mail from this box. Marilyn Osten will apply the payments to the customer accounts, on the computer in the office, through the computer in her home and a telephone connection between the home and the office. The checks will be deposited by Jack or Marilyn.

Dottie will prepare an aged accounts receivable every other day which will be reviewed by Jack Osten. Jack will contact the late customers whose balances are over 30 days old by phone. Follow-up letters, summarizing the conversation, will be sent out the same day or next business day.

Dottie will prepare the accounts payable material for payment and submit this to Jack Osten. Jack will review the material, initial it, and give it to Marilyn Osten who will prepare the checks. All checks will have the amount imprinted into the check to reduce the potential for fraud.

Dottie will prepare the payroll forms based on Lewie Miller's authorization forms. Jack Osten will review the payroll forms, with Lewie's forms, and initial the payroll forms. Marilyn Osten will prepare the payroll checks (with imprinted amounts) and all other payroll reporting data.

Dottie will perform all check reconciliations for accounts payable and payroll systems. Dottie will report any unusual situations to Jack Osten.

EPC - Eastside Plating Company

CONTINGENCIES

Inaccurate Sales Projections

If sales figures are less than projected, we will have to adjust our marketing strategy and/or reduce our expenses. The first thing we will do is to contact the customers who used us once and did not return. We need to find out what, if anything, we did wrong and correct it.

If there are no problems and we have not already started our new customer mailing, we will concentrate on getting a mailing to those potential customers closest to us. We will also follow-up with phone calls a few days later to answer any questions.

If we are not already offering the discounts, e.g. one percent for each $5,000 of orders in a year, we will look at implementing this policy.

Production Costs Become Too High

The basic major production costs are labor, utilities and chemicals. Beginning with labor, we will look at ways to reduce the labor content of our production. We may put some workers on part time, consolidate jobs for greater efficiency and look to getting more through-put from our automatic line.

We will be looking at a system to desalinate the waste water from our water purification system. By doing this we can recycle the waste water and reduce our dependence upon city water.

We will always be looking at vendors who can provide us with the chemicals we need. We may not always purchase our chemicals from the most cost effective vendor. However, we will weigh this in consideration of the other services the vendor provides.

EPC - Eastside Plating Company

Growth Plans

EPC - Eastside Plating Company

FUTURE SERVICES

Other Coatings — We will be looking at black oxide coatings as one way to expand our business.

New Marketplaces — We will be looking at strengthening our relationships with companies who have their own in-house plating shops, e.g. Hallmark, Square D, etc. First, so we can pick up their overload. Second, we want to be in a position to become their vendor of choice should they decide to close their shop.

Exit — Over the next 13 years we will build Eastside Plating Company to be the undisputed second largest plater and polisher in Kansas City. At the end of this time we will sell the company.